DISCERN
THESE
TIMES

By S.I. McMillen, M.D.
NONE OF THESE DISEASES
DISCERN THESE TIMES

A Study Guide to DISCERN THESE TIMES is forthcoming. This will contain questions, appendixes, and reference material with a comprehensive index. References to these appendixes are made throughout this volume, so that students will be better able to use the *Guide* in conjunction with *DISCERN THESE TIMES*.

DISCERN
THESE
TIMES

S.I. McMILLEN, M. D.

17102

FLEMING H. REVELL COMPANY

OLD TAPPAN, NEW JERSEY

SBN 8007–0455–X

Contents

	Foreword	7
1	Discern These Times	11
2	"This Is a Revelation From Jesus Christ"	18
3	Fantastic Space Trip	26
4	Greatest Oratorio of All Time	32
5	United Nations in Prophecy?	39
6	Nuclear Bombs on God's Timetable?	44
7	Courage For the Crisis	52
8	The Time of Satan's Wrath	57
9	The Antichrist Flies Into Action	64
10	When East Clashes With West	69
11	Drugs, Immorality, Crime—All Predicted	76
12	Man's Most Thrilling Day	85
13	Treaty—Temple—Trickster—Tribulation	91
14	Israel—God's Sign in the Sky	98
15	What's Next in the Middle East?	105
16	Daniel's Portrait of the Antichrist	110
17	Will One Nation Rule the World?	116
18	Rejoicing or Remorse?	123
19	God Battles the Antichrist	130
20	Communism Versus Catholicism	138
21	The Woman Rides the Beast	143
22	The Red Beast	148
23	The Victorious Climax	155
24	The Great Day of God's Wrath	163
25	The Millennium	171
26	The Revelation—Golden Dome of the Bible	177

Foreword

Discern These Times speaks to the awareness of modern be-
lievers to current events and the interest in Bible prophecy.
Events discussed in the daily newspapers are connected with the
revealed Word of God. Fulfillments of predictive elements of
Scripture constitute a firm ground for the Divine inspiration of
Scripture and give support to faith in the Scripture.

Prophecy being fulfilled today imparts excitement of expecta-
tion and inspires motivation to meet the prerequisites within the
power of the Christian to hastening the coming of the Lord.
Perhaps the most notable of these prophecies are those concerning the return of Israel to Palestine and the restoration of Jerusalem to the sovereignty of Israel. It took widespread persecution
of world Jewry, World War II, the series of political actions of
Britain, the League of Nations, and the United Nations, the Jew-
ish-Arab Wars of 1948, 1956 and 1967 to bring this to pass, but
fulfillment is here.

The possibility always exists that the great powers will compel
Israel to return some territory taken in war, or to internationalize
Jerusalem and thus, defer this fulfillment. Nevertheless, the state
of affairs today approximates the prophesied events. Some un-
fulfilled prophecies await the unfolding of history, such as the
condition of security of Israel depicted preliminary to the last
invasion of Palestine. We must be aware of the warning of Jesus
that the generation which witnesses the fulfillment of these
things will not pass away before His Advent occurs. The patent
fact is that for the first time in history the prerequisites of the
Second Coming can all be fulfilled in one generation!

My interest was so stimulated by Dr. McMillen's exposition and explanation of Revelation with references to current events that I read the entire book in one day. Many aspects of this prophecy are strikingly fulfilled. Other applications which are made are ingenious (such as the application of the rider on the white horse of Revelation 6 with the United Nations) but are not so ready of proof. Traditionally, the white horse and rider have been taken to represent the spread of the Gospel. Many figures which have usually been considered to be figurative are accepted as literal by Dr. McMillen, such as the 200,000,000 army coming against Israel from the East. Adequate grounds for such literal interpretation are given.

Dr. McMillen exposes the lack of foundation for the placing of the Rapture of believers at the fourth chapter of Revelation. While firmly believing in the Rapture, he shows that it logically comes at the sound of the last or seventh trumpet, or just before the outpouring of the wrath of God. Correctly he points out that the church and Christians will suffer the wrath of men, including the Antichrist, but will be delivered from the wrath of God. This fact is missed by consistent dispensationalists.

The emphasis upon Russia as the source of the Antichrist has much to support it. In fact, the comparison of the Revelation with the word of the Old Testament prophets is quite convincing. The problems of a Millennium with resurrected saints and human beings living side by side are not treated. But Dr. McMillen teaches that the literal Millennium will be on earth.

Whatever one may think of the details of interpretation, he cannot doubt the general trend of meaning of the Revelation after reading *Discern These Times.* The missionary doctor-turned-expositor has much to say on the closing days of the twentieth century.

HAROLD JOHN OCKENGA
Hamilton, Massachusetts

DISCERN
THESE
TIMES

1

DISCERN THESE TIMES

The writings of God's inspired prophets are indispensable in discerning these times. Central in such a study is the Book of Revelation. Its first verse gives the reason:

> This is a Revelation from Jesus Christ, which God gave him
> so that he might show his servants what must very soon take
> place. (Revelation 1:1 PHILLIPS)

No other book in the Bible makes such an outstanding claim for itself. In His Revelation, Jesus Christ permits man to see through His eyes some of the spectacular events of the last days in this age. What a rare privilege!

However, is it not strange that such an unusual "Revelation from Jesus Christ" is sorely neglected in the average Christian circle? Why? To acquire knowledge in any field requires an application that few are willing to give to understand the prophecies of His Word. What a pity since no one can discern the tumultuous times of our day and of the days ahead without an understanding of this, the Lord's Revelation!

Study of prophecy not only helps one to discern the present times and the future, but it also provides facts to support one's faith. Isaiah repeatedly shows that man alone cannot predict future events (Isaiah 41:23; 45:11; 46:9,10; 48:3–7). But Isaiah indicates that God, by predicting events long before they happen, proves both the reality of God's existence and His omniscience!

Likewise today, when man can recognize twentieth century fulfillments of God's ancient prophecies, he then has a solid factual basis for his faith in God and His Word!

Millions of followers in hundreds of other religions have *faith* in idols and gods—as much or more than the average Christian. But none of these man-made religions has *objective facts* to confirm its faith. In contrast, the Christian who has studied the Lord's prophecies and seen their fulfillments in the past and in the present—that person has irrefutable factual basis for his faith in the Lord, the one and only God. Here is one of the remarkable distinctions that sets Christianity at an infinite distance above all human religions and philosophies.

Since the Bible predicts that the last days of this age will be characterized by false teachers, unprecedented iniquity, and a wholesale apostasy of the church (Matthew 24:9–13; 2 Thessalonians 2:1–3), fortunate is that person who can discern in such godless situations solid facts to encourage and give him objective signs to support his faith. But Jesus predicts the state of the undiscerning, the vulnerable Christians: "Sin will be rampant everywhere and will cool the love of many" (Matthew 24:12 LNT).

But blessed and happy is the knowledgeable Christian who sees in this widespread and rapidly growing immorality and apostasy the fulfillment of prophecy. As the times darken, his faith will strengthen.

There is a third reason for studying Revelation. It gives one an intense desire to share his joy with others. Knowing that the time is short, he quadruples his efforts to get the gospel out to the world to hasten his Lord's return (Matthew 24:14). Study of prophecy should light a fire under a lethargic Christian, energize him to do the job that the Lord gave the church to do (28:19,20).

Finally, a fourth reason to study prophecy. What a delight to sit in a grandstand seat with the Lord to view the fulfillments of His predictions in the exciting dramas of this twentieth century! What a thrill to see these age-old predictions, unbattered by the scoffers of the centuries, come to life: (1) The miraculous return of the Jews to their homeland; (2) The rebirth of Israel as an independent nation; (3) The capture of Israel's Golden City, Jerusalem (Ezekiel 37; Matthew 24:3,32,33; Luke 21:24).

What a glorious experience to sit with the Lord in the grandstand of prophecy and cheer for Ezekiel and the Lord Jesus Christ while their prophecies are being fulfilled in this generation. Of course, this experience is an emotional one! But forgivable because it is much akin to the excitement of millions over the world when the first men returned from the moon to the earth right on time and at the right place. Man's greatest technological triumph to that time!

Many Christians have read Ezekiel 37 with its valley of dry bones and the sticks—both symbols representing dispersed Israel. And they also read God's prediction for this scattered nation:

> . . . say to them, Thus says the Lord God: Observe, I am taking
> the children of Israel from among the nations whither they

are gone and will gather them . . . into their own land; and I
will make them one nation in the land. . . . They shall dwell
in the land . . . they and their children and their children's
children forever. . . . (Ezekiel 37:21,22,25 BERKELEY)

What a far-reaching prophecy! And what a miraculous fulfillment in
the return of the Jews to Palestine in the 1940's! One called it, "The
greatest homecoming in history." It was truly that. No nation had ever
been so hopelessly scattered, persecuted, and slaughtered over many
centuries and then returned to their homeland!

Consider the many Christians who were completely thrilled by
the accomplishments of the men who blasted off from the earth, did
their job on the moon, and then returned to the earth right on target. These Christians watched their TV screens and avidly followed
every movement of the men before, during, and after this remarkable
feat.

Yet these Christians forgot that the prophet Ezekiel blasted a mighty
prophecy into space. It streaked through time and space not a few days
as did the astronauts but Ezekiel's prophecy zoomed through time for
2,500 years. What a contrast! Then it fulfilled its mission—landed right
on target in the birth of the nation of Israel—May 14, 1948.

Did Christians read everything in the papers and talk to everybody
about the "landing" in 1948 of this ancient prophecy? Did they? Not
where I was!

Before studying Revelation it would be helpful to realize that many
good Christians have an infidelic quirk, a bizarre hesitancy to really
believe God's prophecies. Because man finds it difficult to recognize
this infidelic trait in himself, it is more acceptable to study it in first-
century believers.

Before Jesus came the first time, the prophets gave hundreds of
accurate details about that advent. Four times to His disciples Jesus
clearly predicted His crucifixion and resurrection (Matthew 12:40; 16:-
21; 17:22,23; 20:17–19). "But they understood not this saying . . ."
(Luke 9:45 KJV).

Repeatedly He told His twelve apostles that He would be crucified
and then rise from the dead on the third day. Yet of these apostles, one
reads, "And they understood none of these things . . ." (Luke 18:34
KJV). If they had, they would not have scattered when Jesus was arrested. Peter would not have denied His Lord with cursing.

They could not accept what Jesus told them because their minds
were full of their own preconceived ideas of what the Messiah would
do. They expected fully to see Jesus on a throne, never on a cross. The
pleasant prospect of sitting in high government positions dominated

13

their thinking. Hence, they were not conditioned to accept the unpleasant aspects of Jesus' teaching.

Man should ever remember that his unconscious *desires* determine in a large measure what he *believes* about prophecy. That principle applies to many another area of thought. One should be very careful about drawing any conclusion if one's desires are helping to shape it.

The apostles were so completely confused by Jesus' crucifixion that they never remembered that He also predicted that He would arise. But the unbelieving Jews remembered and asked Pilate to give them soldiers to guard the tomb.

Hence, on the third day when Jesus stated He would arise, the apostles were snoring away. Some dear women—bless their good intentions—went to the tomb to anoint His *dead* body. In the tomb they saw two angels who said:

> . . . "Why are you looking in a tomb for someone who is alive? He isn't here! He has come back to life again! Don't you remember what He told you . . . that the Messiah must be betrayed . . . and be crucified and that He would arise . . . the third day?"
>
> Then they remembered. And returned to Jerusalem and told His eleven disciples—and everyone else—what had happened . . .
>
> But the story sounded like a fairy tale to the men—they didn't believe it. (Luke 24:5–11 LNT)

They didn't believe it. Even after the "responsible" masculine sex had seen the empty tomb, their preconceived ideas kept them from believing.

Two of these discouraged disciples trudged toward Emmaus. When the unrecognized Jesus joined them and asked why they were sad, they bewailed the woeful story of the crucifixion. They groaned, "We had thought He was the glorious Messiah . . ." (24:21 LNT). *We had thought.* They had buried all their hopes in the tomb.

> Then Jesus said to them, "You are such foolish, foolish people! You find it so hard to believe all that the prophets wrote in the Scriptures! (24:25 LNT)

We had thought. Both the disciples and the Jewish scholars regarded the crucifixion as proving that Jesus had no valid claim to be the Messiah. Yet seven centuries before, Isaiah and the prophets predicted a host of minute details about that crucifixion. No wonder Jesus singed them, "You find it so hard to believe all that the prophets wrote in the Scriptures." The Lord expects Christians today to know and to expect that His prophecies will be fulfilled to the letter.

In fact, in the twenty-four hours of the Lord's betrayal and crucifixion twenty-five specific prophecies were fulfilled. (See *Guide,* Appendix 1 for these remarkable predictions.)

How could these twenty-five fulfillments of prophecy occur in such a short period of a man's life unless he were the Messiah? A mathematician figured there would be only one chance in 33,000,000 of this being a coincidence, declares Newman Watts in *The Incomparable Book.*

Furthermore, Watts states that in the whole life, crucifixion, and resurrection of the Lord, 333 prophecies were fulfilled! Every one of these gives factual evidence that Jesus was the predicted Messiah.

Jesus did not expect His disciples to know all of these 333 predictions that related to His first coming but He scorched them because they failed to believe what they did know. Since there are several times as many more predictions that relate to His second coming, what would He say to His undiscerning, disbelieving followers in this truly exciting conclusion of the twentieth century?

Another time Jesus rebuked His followers, ". . . You are good at reading the weather signs of the skies . . . but you can't read the obvious signs of the times!" (Matthew 16:2,3 LNT). Today man has many sophisticated instruments to predict the weather, even spatial satellites, yet modern man is pathetically unaware of the many signs of His return mentioned by the prophets and by Jesus Christ in the Gospels and in His Revelation.

Three have already been mentioned: (1) the return of the Jews; (2) the rebirth of Israel and (3) the capture of Jerusalem.

Consider two signs that the Lord gave that Christians might recognize the approximate time of His return to this earth. Here is the first: ". . . in the time of the coming of the Son of Man, life will be as it was in the days of Noah" (Luke 17:26 PHILLIPS). The Bible specifies what life was like in Noah's day: ". . . the wickedness of man was great . . . every imagination of the thoughts of his heart was only evil continually. . . . The earth also was corrupt before God, and the earth was filled with violence" (Genesis 6:5,11 KJV). Violence is also emphasized in verse 13.

Observe the second sign that Jesus gives: "It [Life] will be just the same as it was in the days of Lot . . ." (Luke 17:28 PHILLIPS). Lot's day was characterized by widespread sexual promiscuity, rape, homosexuality, lawlessness, and violence (Genesis 19).

The Apostle Peter also predicts what the last days of this age will be:

15

"First, I want to remind you that in the last days will come scoffers who will do every wrong that they can think of . . ." (2 Peter 3:3 LNT). Wickedness will only be limited by the depths of the cesspools of their imaginations. How similar to the last third of this century!

The Apostle Paul also portrays an ugly picture of the last days:

> You may as well know this too, Timothy, that in the last days it is going to be very difficult to be a Christian.
>
> For people . . . will be disobedient to their parents, ungrateful to them, and thoroughly bad.
>
> . . . they will be constant liars and troublemakers and will think nothing of immorality . . .
>
> They will go to church, yes, but they won't really believe anything they hear . . .
>
> They are the kind who craftily sneak into other people's homes and make friendships with silly, sin-burdened women . . .
>
> In fact, evil men and false teachers will become worse and worse, deceiving many, they themselves having been deceived by Satan. (2 Timothy 3:1–6,13 LNT)

Of course, immoral practices have existed from the fall of man. But the utter depravity described in detail by Jesus, Peter, and Paul is much different, far worse, and beyond control.

Modern man has been plagued in some measure by the evils detailed by these three prophets. In some measure! But between 1965 and 1970 it seemed that somewhere a moral dam gave way and the resulting flood has played havoc with civilization *in a measure never before recorded in history*. Never before has civilization approximated so closely all the details predicted by Jesus, Peter, and Paul.

Secular observers also recognize that the 1965–1970 period came without precedents or antecedents, as lightning out of the blue. Although John Brooks authored a book in 1965 covering the events of the previous twenty-five years, he felt that the 1965–1970 period ushered in such a startling new era that he depicted it in an article with the jolting title, "A Clean Break With the Past" (*American Heritage*, August, 1970).

Instead of the small but steady decline of moral values seen in this century, one was amazed to observe that in this five year period there was a sharp almost precipitous drop. Certain groups could not drop any lower. They met every one of the many details predicted for the last days of this age. Perhaps conditions are not as widespread as they will be, but they are rapidly spreading.

16

In this five year period one observed widespread legalized pornography; wife-swapping; nudity; sexual promiscuity; nude obscene performances both in movies and on the stage; acceptance by churches of homosexuality; co-ed dormitories; college distribution of the "pill" to all women who ask for it; abortion on demand legalized in New York state; loud demands for divorce on demand without any questions or waiting period; rock festivals attended by tens of thousands permitting nudity, sexual performances, and sale of drugs many with no police interference; communes housing thousands with venereal diseases, a rate five to ten times higher than the local rates; universities forced to choose between shutting down or being burned down; a nation with military commitments yet the government compelled to close its recruiting and officer training centers on campus; blowing up of University of Wisconsin science building; the nation's young men burning their draft cards and their country's flag; wholesale desertion from the armed forces; the spectacle of national political conventions being held behind high barricades and protected by police; blocks of city houses burned down and shooting of firemen; widespread use of drugs which scramble the brains of university students at home and soldiers in Viet Nam; radicals convicted of crimes, who appeal, are set free, become national heroes, and tour the country to spread violence; and so on, *ad infinitum!*

It is well recognized that these powerful forces are seeking to destroy the foundations of Christianity. Radical leaders gleefully predict that since few young people are becoming pillars in the church, her collapse is not far away. Soon the Gospel of Christ will be replaced by their teachings of Karl Marx. The dedication and energy of the radical groups will succeed unless Christians become possessed with the greater power of the Holy Spirit manifested in the first century.

Also, the church must give to both young and old factual foundations for their faith, just as Jesus and His Spirit-filled apostles pointed out the signs and fulfillments in their day.

As a teen-ager I vividly recall a book that fortified me in the university with objective proofs of the inspiration of the Bible. The title was *Nelson on Infidelity.* In later years the study of the Old Testament prophets and their fulfillment as recorded in history greatly confirmed my faith in God's Word.

In recent years the study of the Revelation of "the last days," enthralled me because of its spectacular relevancy to the trends of the closing days of this century. Just as God gave many infallible proofs in the fulfillments of prophecies relating to Jesus' First Coming, He is miraculously fulfilling today many prophecies relating to His Second Coming—and purposely so in order to counteract today's recent and particularly virulent attacks on the church! These prophecies and their fulfillments will shortly be detailed in this study of His Revelation. Let all pray that the incredible disbelief of first-century disciples may not be repeated in His followers today.

Before beginning this study—one final word. Even though the disciples and apostles had the best instruction on the events of their day, yet they miserably failed to discern the times. When Jesus was arrested and other predictions began to be fulfilled, they fled. Why? The Lord knew they needed the power and the mental illumination that only the indwelling Holy Spirit could give (John 14:26; Acts 1:8; 2:16–18;-38–41). When Peter received the Holy Spirit at Pentecost, he was not only able to discern for the first time everything that the Lord and the prophets had predicted but the Holy Spirit gave to him and to other apostles the important ability to relate these predictions to their own time.

The Apostle Paul explained that the natural man ". . . can't understand and can't accept these thoughts from God, which the Holy Spirit teaches us. They sound foolish to him, because only those who have the Holy Spirit within them can understand what the Holy Spirit means. Others just can't take it in" (1 Corinthians 2:14 LNT).

Here is the reason the disciples and apostles of Jesus could not understand the prophecies before they were filled with the Holy Spirit. As one studies the Revelation, let him constantly seek that precious discernment that only the Holy Spirit can give.

2

"THIS IS A REVELATION FROM JESUS CHRIST"

Revelation 1

Startling events of this century only thrill the student of prophecy. Frightening news headlines strengthen the knowledgeable Christian.

He is not depressed by the threat of another world war with the probability of nuclear bombs. Neither is he cast down by the widespread apostasy in the church nor by the international spread of Communism. He deplores, yes, but is not discouraged by the collapse of morality. To one versed in the Bible, these situations are clear signs of the promised return of his Lord.

Best suited to discern these times is this "Revelation from Jesus Christ." No book in the Word claims as much for itself as the first words of chapter 1 of Revelation:

> This is a Revelation from Jesus Christ . . . (PHILLIPS)
> This is the Revelation given by God to Jesus Christ. (NEB)
> A revelation by Jesus Christ . . . (MOFFATT)

To sense that this book is truly "a Revelation from Jesus Christ" is to take off one's shoes before reading. After such a claim, one can understand why Jamieson, Fausset and Brown wrote in *Commentary on the Whole Bible*, "Jesus Christ, not John the writer, is the Author of the Apocalypse." And William Barclay declared in *The Revelation of John* that "This is not the Revelation which tells *about* Jesus Christ, but the Revelation which was given by Jesus Christ."

Agreeing with these views are authorities of note: A.T. Robertson, H.B. Swete, J.B. Smith, John Wesley, Hanns Lilje, and R.F. Weymouth. Of course, the other books of the Bible are divinely inspired yet only Revelation claims to be divinely authored.

In this connection one should recall that the Apostle Paul is properly considered the author of Romans. Yet Tertius wrote it (Romans 16:22). Paul is considered the author, the originator of the concepts, just as Jesus should be in the composition of the Book of Revelation.

> This is a Revelation from Jesus Christ . . . (1:1 PHILLIPS). God permitted Him to reveal these things to His servant John in a vision; and then an angel was sent from heaven to explain the vision's meaning. John wrote it all down—the words of God and Jesus Christ and everything he heard and saw. (1:1,2 LNT)

Twenty-eight times John declares, "I heard." Twelve times he is told, "Write." Once he began to write down what the seven thunders said, but a voice reined him up, "Write not!" Today no secretary has as close supervision as did the Apostle John.

However on thirty-eight occasions, the Lord unveiled moving dramas which John described with his own words. But even here he could hardly be called the author, since this word means *originator.* He acted as a reporter, but one should add, a meticulously accurate reporter.

This book is unique in not having "a single formal quotation" from the Old Testament as A.T. Robertson writes in *Word Pictures in the New Testament*. Since it is a Revelation from Jesus Christ it would be illogical for Him to quote from mortal man to prove a divine assertion.

However, this book has nearly four hundred allusions to the Old Testament (See H.S. Miller's *General Biblical Introduction*.)—almost equal to all the rest of the New Testament. To skillfully weave these hundreds of allusions into such a short book as Revelation is a clear indication of the supernatural knowledge of its Author. And to think that these allusions are from twenty-five different books of the Old Testament, according to H.B. Swete in *The Apocalypse of John*!

Reading any part of God's inspired Word will surely bless mind, body, and soul; but only this book promises a special blessing to him who reads and obeys it.

> If you read this prophecy aloud to the church, you will receive a special blessing from the Lord. Those who listen to it being read and do what it says will also be blessed. For the time is near when these things will all come true. (1:3 LNT)

This is the first of seven beatitudes (Revelation 1:3; 14:13; 16:15; 19:9; 20:6; 22:7,14).

For the time is near. (See *Guide*, Appendix 2 for elaboration.)

This book is unique from all other books. Here, as one would expect from its divine authorship, the salutation is from all the members of the Trinity:

> John, to the seven churches in Asia: Grace and peace to you from Him who is and who was and who is coming, from the seven Spirits before His throne, and from Jesus Christ the faithful witness, firstborn of the dead, and ruler of kings upon earth. (1:5 PHILLIPS)

Who is and who was and who is coming. Since He is the One on the throne, the Father must be in view here. Both the Father and the Son will return to this earth (6:16; 20:11).

The seven Spirits. The seven Spirits symbolize the infinite power of the Holy Spirit to do anything, anytime, and anywhere.

Seven churches . . . seven Spirits. This book is saturated with fifty-nine occurrences of *seven* and *seventh.* From Genesis to Revelation the number *seven* symbolizes completion or infinity. *Seven churches* signifies every church in every country and in every generation.

From Jesus Christ the faithful witness. Where could a more reliable witness be found to substantiate this book?

Firstborn of the dead. In His resurrection, Jesus was the first to live again. And He promised, ". . . because I live, ye shall live also" (John 14:19 KJV). With such a Lord and with such a promise, death can hold no fear!

Ruler of kings upon earth. Fierce battles occur in this book but always one is cheered to see the ultimate triumph of our Lord.

Not only in the future but here and now blessings are promised:

> To Him who loves us and freed us from our sins with His life's
> blood, who made of us a royal house, to serve as the priests of
> his God and Father—to him be glory and dominion forever
> and ever! Amen. (1:5,6 NEB)

Jesus loves us. To know that there is a "friend that sticketh closer than a brother" (Proverbs 18:24 KJV) is to soar above despair and depression—the most common factor in emotional upsets. Our gratitude for His love if expressed in praise and song has wonderful therapeutic value.

Freed us from our sins. Physicians know that about two-thirds of our physical and emotional symptoms stem from the carnal emotions of jealousy, envy, self-centeredness, resentment, anger, and guilt. To be free from our sins and these disease-producing emotions will truly give real vitality to every bit of life.

Today many professed Christians are ashamed of their Lord. Some day that shame will turn to fear:

> See! He is arriving surrounded by clouds; and every eye shall
> see Him—yes, and those who pierced Him. And the nations
> will weep in sorrow and in terror when He comes. Yes! Amen!
> Let it be so! (1:7 LNT)

To the salutation from the Trinity is added the divine signature:

"I am the A and Z, the Beginning and the Ending of all things," says God, who is the Lord, the All Powerful One who is, and was, and is coming again! (1:8 LNT)

The All Powerful One (The Almighty). Nine of the ten occurrences of the Greek word rendered *Almighty* occur in Revelation. Why? Since this book is beamed to a persecuted group, they need to be constantly reminded that only God is Almighty. Their godless rulers are here today and gone tomorrow.

The next verse gives a clue why the Lord picked John to pen this book:

It is I, your brother John, a fellow sufferer for the Lord's sake who is writing this letter to you. I too have shared the patience Jesus gives, and we will share His kingdom! I was on the island of Patmos, exiled there ... for telling what I knew about Jesus Christ. (1:9 LNT)

Introducing himself simply as John is strong evidence that the widely known apostle is the scribe. (See *Guide*, Appendix 3.)

Exiled for telling what I knew about Jesus Christ. The crime of witnessing for Christ has ever been in some countries a heinous offense. The time of this writing is about A.D. 90 during the reign of Domitian, said to be more beastly than the infamous Nero.

But the days are coming when such witnessing will be punishable by death throughout the world (6:9; 7:9–14). This Book of Revelation is a book of cheer to help persecuted Christians in every generation but especially those living under the Antichrist.

Patmos is one of many volcanic islands west of Turkey—rocky, treeless, barren, and uninviting. Sir William Ramsay, in William Barclay's *The Revelation of John* suggests that John's banishment was characterized by "scourging, marked by perpetual fetters, scanty clothing, insufficient food, sleep on the bare ground, a dark prison and work under the lash of a military overseer."

How long would today's chocolate Christian last in such a place? Did this ninety-year-old apostle succumb to self-pity? He gives three ingredients in his prescription for this common ailment:

1 The patience which Jesus gives (v.9)
2 Anticipation of the coming glorious kingdom (v.9)
3 Inspiration of the Holy Spirit (v.10)

This prescription has miracle action to prevent mental distress.

I was exiled on Patmos. Taken in the right attitude, misfortune can become a blessing. Because John was separated from his friends, he could hear God speak clearly without any human static. Likewise, Paul did not receive his unusual revelations from God until he exiled himself to the Arabian desert.

> The gospel I preach to you is no human invention. No man gave it to me, no man taught it to me . . . I did not even go to Jerusalem to meet those who were God's messengers before me—no, I went away to Arabia. . . . (Galatian 1:11–17 PHILLIPS)

Is it a coincidence that John the Baptist and the apostles John and Paul were in lonely wildernesses when they received their remarkable revelations from God? And could it be that our understanding of God's prophetic revelations depends on the degree to which we screen out the chatter of earthly voices, newspapers, magazine, radio, and television?

John now describes the first vision that he sees:

> On the Lord's day I knew myself inspired by the Spirit, and I heard behind me a voice loud as a trumpet call, saying, "Write down in a book what you see and send it to the seven churches . . . !"
> I turned to see whose voice it was that was speaking to me, and when I turned I saw seven golden lampstands, and among these lampstands I saw someone like a Son of Man. . . . (1:-10–13 PHILLIPS)

On this Lord's day John's thought had probably been riveted on spiritual values—certainly not on the trivial nor the doubtful. God can only bless those who are tuned to His thoughts. Only then can they hear the voice and perceive the Son of man.

Like a Son of man. The definite article is not in the Greek. The emphasis is on the humanity of Jesus. He identifies Himself with the poor and persecuted. Very much a man, yet God!

He is "among these lampstands," symbols of the churches (v.20). How comforting to remember that Christ is ever watching over His bride the Church, identifying with them as a Son of man.

The same Lord was with the Hebrew children in the fiery furnace, but in a different role. There He is called "the Son of God," perhaps, because He demonstrated His sovereign power to deliver them *from* the fiery furnace. But in Revelation His characteristic title is "the slain Lamb," a constant reminder to Christians of His attitude *during* persecution.

But in this opening chapter, John sees His glorified Lord:

> ... I saw ... one like unto a son of man, clothed with a garment down to the foot, and girt about at the breasts with a golden girdle. And his head and his hair were white as white wool, white as snow; and his eyes were as a flame of fire; and his feet like unto burnished brass, as if it had been refined in a furnace; and his voice as the voice of many waters. And he had in his right hand seven stars: and out of his mouth proceeded a sharp two-edged sword: and his countenance was as the sun shineth in his strength. (1:12–16 ASV)

Here is a beautiful example of the glorious language of this book, language replete with symbolism. (To understand this universal language see *Guide,* Appendix 4.) In this passage "white" is a symbol of His purity and eternal nature (See also Daniel 7:9; Isaiah 1:18).

His eyes were as a flame of fire. (Compare Daniel 10:6). Here is vision that burns through human excuses to reveal the hidden cancer of the soul. He sees what closest friends never suspected. "... everything lies naked and exposed to the eyes of the One with whom we have to reckon" (Hebrew 4:13 NEB). At the judgment such insight will reveal and burn away the alibis of straw.

His feet like burnished brass! Brass is a common symbol of judgment. Such feet pulverize all opposition.

His voice as the sound of many waters. In a later vision (Revelation 17:15), John is told that "many waters" symbolizes "peoples and multitudes and nations and tongues."

In His right hand seven stars. The right hand symbolizes the infinite power and loving proximity of the Lord to the seven stars, symbols of the churches over the world.

When I saw Him, I fell at His feet as dead ... (1:17 BERKELEY). Here was someone so different and awesome that John was terrified. There was no recognition of the mild-mannered Jesus who John knew in the flesh. If John had been copying descriptions given by prophets, he would not have fallen down in terror. John was describing a vision that the Lord revealed to *him.* John's reaction was similar to others who had seen members of the Godhead.

. . . Then He laid His right hand on me and said, Do not fear! I am the First and the Last and the Living One, I experienced death and behold, I am alive forever and ever, (Amen), and I possess the keys of death and its realm. (1:17,18 BERKELEY)

Before the stars were, Jesus was (Colossians 1:17). After world dictators become dust and the heavens vanish, He will still be the Lord of all.

I possess the keys of death. Why should the Christian fear firing squads and gas chambers if their Master has the keys of death? His resurrection proved that He does. Again one sees the purpose of this book—to condition the Christian for coming persecution.

Note the instructions that John the reporter receives:

Write down what you have just seen, and what soon will be shown to you. (1:19 LNT)

Write each vision down while it is still fresh in your mind.

Most of the many symbols in this first vision were comprehensible, but two needed clarification:

As to the mystery of the seven stars upon My right hand, and of the seven golden lampstands—the seven stars are angels of the seven churches, and the seven lampstands are the seven churches. (1:20 BERKELEY)

Forty-six symbols in Revelation are explained in the book itself, according to J.B. Smith in *A Revelation of Jesus Christ.* The first two are that the stars are the angels caring for seven churches, and the lampstands are symbols of the churches. One should engrave these beautiful symbols on the mind! (See *Guide,* Appendix 5.)

(Chapters two and three of Revelation record seven epistles that the Lord dictated to seven churches in John's day. Seven is symbolical of the universality and the eternal values of these epistles—applicable to all churches everywhere and in all ages. Therefore, all should read and reread these invaluable letters. Not only must one understand what the Lord has dictated here but one must adjust his spiritual life to the divine directives in order to obtain the promised blessings.)

Because the language of these epistles is clear, this author feels that no commentary is needed to fulfill the purpose of his book. However, Revelation 2 and 3 do form an essential part of the structure of the book as a whole. (The fascinating outline of the Revelation is given in *Guide,* Appendix 6.)

3

FANTASTIC SPACE TRIP

Revelation 4

A Russian astronaut after orbiting the earth pronounced this crudity, "I didn't see God up there." The Apostle John not only saw God but viewed His glorious throne and many other wonderful sights. John describes what few mortals ever saw—our future home:

> Then as I looked, I saw a door standing open in heaven, and the same voice I had heard before, that sounded like a mighty trumpet blast, spoke to me and said,
> "Come up here and I will show you what must happen in the future!"
> And instantly I was, in spirit, there in heaven and saw—oh the glory of it!—a throne and Someone sitting on it!
> Great bursts of light flashed forth from Him as from a glittering diamond, or from a shining ruby, and a rainbow glowing like an emerald encircled His throne. (4:1–3 LNT)

A few others have seen and portrayed the glories of heaven: Moses and the seventy Elders (Exodus 24:9–11,17); Isaiah (Isaiah 6:1–4); Ezekiel (Ezekiel 1:25–28); Daniel (Daniel 7:9,10); and Stephen (Acts 7:55,56).

These men had difficulty in describing the glory scenes with an earthly vocabulary. They likened the exquisite colors to the most precious jewels they had ever seen. The form of God was not sharply outlined because of the blinding brilliance emanating from His throne.

Imagine the most striking and exquisite sunset you ever saw; raise that beauty to the nth degree. *That's* a small bit of heaven! Visualize a sapphire lake bordered by thousands of trees adorned in a riot of autumnal glory. *That's* a mere sample of the beauty that awaits the overcomer.

Years ago, on my first plane ride, I left Buffalo on a dark snowy day. Never shall I forget my thrill and excitement when I emerged into the dazzling sunshine above the silver-lined clouds. To me it was an entirely new and glorious dimension—a tiny foretaste of heaven.

Now I can appreciate the much greater excitement that John felt when he flew up from dreary Patmos and viewed the fantastic wonders of heaven itself. A.T. Robertson in *Word Pictures in the New Testament* and J.B. Phillips in *The Book of Revelation* state that the apostle, because of the intense emotion of being in heaven and trying to describe the fabulous scenes before him, would naturally have a different style to that used when he quietly penned his gospel record.

Some of this glory rubbed off on J.B. Phillips as he translated the Book of Revelation. In the Introduction he writes:

> . . . For in this book the translator is carried into another dimension—he has but the slightest foothold in the time-and-space world with which he is familiar. He is carried, not into some never-never land of fancy, but into the ever-ever land of God's eternal Values and Judgments . . . the writer, who had a genuine ecstatic experience, wrote down what he saw *during the visions*. The intense emotion of being as it were, "in the heavenlies," the excitement of seeing what is normally invisible to human eyes, and the frustration of having to use human words to describe what is beyond human expression would, it seems to me, fully account for the incoherence, the strange formation of sentences, the repetition, and the odd juxtaposition of words. If we suppose this to be true . . . then we can reasonably imagine that he would shrink from correction or revision lest he distort or modify the revelation he had been given.

Is it not thrilling that even this change in John's style and diction supports the credibility of this book?

After looking at God and His throne, John then proceeds to describe other heavenly personages:

> Twenty-four smaller thrones surrounded His with twenty-four elders sitting on them; all were clothed in white, with golden crowns upon their heads.
>
> Lightning and thunder issued from the throne, and there were voices in the thunder. Directly in front of His throne were seven lighted lamps representing the seven-fold Spirit of God. (4:4,5 LNT)

These Elders are frequently mentioned in this book, but nowhere is their identity revealed. Scholars believe they are symbolic of the redeemed for these reasons:

1 Both are arrayed in white (Revelation 3:4,5,18; 7:13,14; 19:8).
2 Both sit on thrones (Matthew 19:27–29; Revelation 3:21; 4:4).
3 Both have harps (Revelation 5:8; 14:2; 15:2).
4 Both wear crowns (Revelation 2:10; 3:11; 4:4).
5 Their activities concern the saints and their redemption (Revelation 5:5,9; 7:13; 11:16–18; 14:3).

(For symbolism of the number 24 see *Guide*, Appendix 7.)

Lightning and thunder issued from the throne. These are common symbols of God's power, His method of commanding attention, and His judgments upon disobedience (1 Samuel 2:10; 7:10; Job 26:14; Revelation 8:5; 10:3,4; 11:19; 16:18; 19:6).

Seven lighted lamps representing the seven-fold Spirit of God. Literally, it is the seven Spirits of God. Zechariah also equated seven lamps with God's Holy Spirit (Zechariah 4:2,6). Seven Spirits emphasize the infinite capabilities of the Holy Spirit.

The next personages whom John sees are, next to Deity, the most important beings in Heaven.

> Spread out before the throne was a shiny crystal sea. Four Living Beings, dotted front and back with eyes, stood at the throne's four sides.
>
> The first of these Living Beings was in the form of a lion; the second looked like an ox; the third had the face of a man; and the fourth, the form of an eagle, with wings spread out as though in flight.
>
> Each of these Living Beings had six wings, and the central sections of their wings were covered with eyes. Day after day and night after night they kept on saying, "Holy, holy, Lord God Almighty—the One who was, and is, and is to come."
> (Revelation 4:6–8 LNT)

Four Living Beings. These are the most holy, the most powerful and the most intriguing of all in God's creation. They stand on the four sides of God's throne. John will mention these repeatedly in this and in later chapters. (See Appendix 8 for discussion of their name.)

The great number of "eyes" over their bodies and wings symbolize the vast extent of their knowledge.

The first was in the form of a lion. Perhaps this one, resembling the king of the beasts, represents the wild animal kingdom before the throne of God. *The second looked like an ox.* He may understand and represent all of the domesticated animals. *The third had the face of a man. The last one had the form of an eagle.* Could he be the representative of every feathered creature? These are the preferred views but others are also given. (See *Guide,* Appendix 9.)

John was not the first prophet to see these "four Living Beings." Ezekiel saw them and gave a two-chapter report (Ezekiel 1 and 10). When he first saw them, he did not know what to call them. As John did, he simply called them "Living Beings." But a year later, he saw them again and wrote, ". . . I recognized them as cherubim . . . they were of the same appearance; they were the same . . ." (Ezekiel 10:20,22 BERKELEY).

Both John and Ezekiel state that there are four Living Beings. They describe their faces as those of a lion, ox, man, and eagle, but perhaps because Ezekiel saw them in motion, he discovered that each one had each of the four faces. But John, seeing them standing still, could only see one face—the one facing him. This important difference indicates that John did not copy Ezekiel's report.

Both prophets were impressed by the great number of eyes on the bodies of the cherubim. John states that they had six wings. Ezekiel records four wings but quickly adds that under their wings was a pair of human hands, making a total of six upper appendages.

Isaiah was another prophet who saw these Living Beings. He, too, was at a loss to know what to call them. Because one of them touched his mouth with a burning coal, he called them by the Hebrew name *seraphim.* If translated, this word is in English "burners." He, as did John, counted six wings. Both he and John report the same acclamation of these beings to their Creator, "Holy, holy, holy." This utterance is found nowhere else in the Bible.

All three prophets show that these Living Beings are close to the throne, are closely associated with fire, and are intermediaries between God and man.

It is important to observe the similarity in the descriptions of Isaiah, Ezekiel, and John:

1 Same name—Living Beings (Ezekiel and John).
2 Their close proximity to God (Isaiah, Ezekiel, and John).
3 Their close association with fire (Isaiah and Ezekiel).
4 The similarity of their chant, "Holy, holy, holy," found nowhere else in Scripture (Isaiah and John).
5 The number of the beings as four (Ezekiel and John).
6 Faces associated with a lion, ox, man, and eagle (Ezekiel and John).
7 Six upper extremities (Isaiah, Ezekiel, and John).
8 The great number of eyes (Ezekiel and John).
9 Their intermediary function (Isaiah, Ezekiel, and John).

In the descriptions of these three prophets there are no irreconcilable differences. The differences result from the prophets seeing these beings perform varied functions. The differences also indicate that these prophets did not copy from each other but were independent observers.

The similarites indicate that each of these prophets did see these four wonderful Living Beings in heaven. Such a conclusion gives factual credibility to the predictions which follow in the Book of Revelation.

Others, including Jamieson and his co-authors William Barclay and Charles R. Erdman, have equated the Living Beings with the cherubim and seraphim. Charles R. Erdman, Professor Emeritus of Princeton Theological Seminary, wraps it all up in this neat package in *Revelation of John:*

> Closely associated with the throne, circling about it, are "four living creatures," which unite the features of the cherubim and the seraphim . . . They represent the highest order of beings.
> . . .

The first mention of these Living Beings or cherubim is found in Genesis 3:24 where God placed them at the gate of Eden to keep disobedient man from entering. This function of separating sinful man from God is repeatedly seen in the construction of the ark and tabernacle. The veil separating the priests from the Holy of Holies was interwoven with cherubim. The High Priest could enter this sacred enclosure only once a year. Even he was separated from God who dwelt between golden cherubim (2 Kings 19:15; 1 Chronicles 13:6; Psalm 80:1; Isaiah 37:16).

These four Living Beings perform at least five outstanding duties, often as intermediaries between God and man.

1 They separate sinful man from a holy God (Genesis 3:24). This function is symbolized in Exodus 25:18–22; 26:1,31.
2 They burn out impurities in man (Isaiah 6:6,7).
3 They transport God's throne (Ezekiel 10:1).
4 They will play strategic roles in events still future on this earth (Revelation 6:1,3,5,7; 15:7).
5 They initiate worship in heaven (Revelation 4:9–11; 5:14).

The last verses of this chapter illustrate their role in initiating worship in heaven.

And when the Living Beings give glory and honor and thanks to the One sitting on the throne, who lives forever and ever,

The twenty-four elders fall down before Him and worship Him, the Eternal Living One, and cast their crowns before the throne saying,

"Oh Lord, You are worthy to receive the glory and the honor and the power, for you have created all things. They were created and called into being by Your act of will. (4:9–11 LNT)

How fitting and beautiful to call these four most holy of God's creations "Living Beings," as is done in such translations as Berkeley and Living New Testament. Other modern translations refer to them as "Living Creatures." But to call them "beasts," as in the King James Version, is unpardonable. In the many references to these Living Beings, John always used the Greek word *dzoon,* a living creature. In contrast, when John repeatedly referred to the Antichrist and his False Prophet he always used a distinctly different Greek word, *therion,* "a wild beast," as is explained in Young's *Analytical Concordance.*

The prophet Ezekiel also referred to them as living creatures in his first encounters with them. But after he discovered that they were the same as the cherubim (Ezekiel 10:20–22), he repeatedly called them cherubim.

These very holy Living Beings are mentioned 127 times in the Bible from Genesis to Revelation with a variety of names in good translations:

Cherub (singular) or cherubim (plural)	91 times
Hebrew *seraphim.* If translated, "burners."	2 times
Living Beings or Creatures in Ezekiel	14 times
Living Beings or Creatures in Revelation	20 times
	127 times

Are Ezekiel's "wheels" to be equated with the Living Beings? For those interested in further study, see *Guide,* Appendix 10. For a summary of the fifth cherub who fell from grace see *Guide,* Appendix 21.

What purpose does Revelation 4 serve in a book of prophecy? This view of God on His throne, with great bursts of flashing colors more beautiful than precious gems, should convince all that God is very much alive today. Such a God certainly knows what is ahead.

Then the seven lamps before His throne emitting the penetrating light of the Holy Spirit warns all that no sin can be hid in any dark recess of the soul. But thanks be to the Lord who died to cleanse every trace of any sin from the heart of the penitent.

The four awe-inspiring Living Beings, continuously emphasizing the holiness of God, should make all cry out with Isaiah, "Woe is me! For I am undone; because I am a man of unclean lips . . . for mine eyes have seen the King, Jehovah of hosts" (Isaiah 6:5 ASV).

After seeing the remarkable similarity of John's descriptions of these heavenly beings to the records of Isaiah and Ezekiel, one has even further reason to accept the credibility of John's predictions in later chapters. This similarity without any of the hallmarks of copying or collusion is a solid foundational fact to strengthen one's faith.

Now one can believe in the predictions of the future with a faith buttressed by facts! In His day the Lord did not expect the people would believe in Him with naked faith but gave them a multiplicity of outstanding signs to support their faith.

Why does one get a view of the twenty-four Elders with crowns on their heads and thrones to sit on? This is a symbolic and encouraging picture of the blessings and honors that God will give to His followers.

Chapters 4 and 5 prepare the mind and the heart to more thoroughly rely on the sure word of prophecy,—so truly relevant to *discern these times.*

4

GREATEST ORATORIO OF ALL TIME

Revelation 5

This chapter is full of music, dramatic and profound:

> I also saw upon the right hand of Him who was seated on the throne a scroll with writing inside and outside, sealed with seven seals. I further saw a mighty angel, who was exclaiming in a loud voice, "Who is worthy to open the scroll and to break its seals?" And no one, either in heaven or on earth or under the earth, was able to open the scroll or to inspect it. (5:1–3 BERKELEY)

What a spectacular "heavenorama!" The Lord of Hosts sitting on a throne is the central figure. The scroll is not clutched *in* His hand but *upon* the open palm to symbolize His eagerness to share this Book of Revelation with others. The *right* hand suggests priority and importance.

Writing inside and outside. Nothing more is to be added to this scroll. Since then religions and cults have added prophetic writings to this scroll, oblivious to the curse that hangs low over their heads (22:18).

The seven unbroken seals indicate authenticity without any prior tampering. These seals rule out John's obtaining his ideas from other prophets or from the wisdom of this world. Yet it is strange how frequently some commentators would have one think that John obtained his ideas from this or that prophet.

Some scholars believe that "the mighty angel" was Gabriel who ordered Daniel to seal a book of prophecy (Daniel 12:4). Certainly Gabriel more than any other angel has been a revealer of prophetic truth (Daniel 8:16; 9:21–27; 10:12–21; 11:2; Luke 1:13–20,26–37).

This angel must have had a powerful voice to reach everyone in heaven, on earth, and under the earth. Although all heard, yet no one accepted the challenge to break the seals.

When no one stepped forward to break the seals, John wept:

> So I cried bitterly because none was found worthy to open the book or to inspect it. And one of the elders said to me, "Do not weep. You see, the Lion out of the tribe of Judah, the Offspring of David, has conquered, so as to open the scroll and (to loose) its seven seals. (5:4,5 BERKELEY)

John's grief was irreconcilable. It did not stem from idle curiosity but from an intense innate desire to transmit its predictions to the seven churches (Revelation 1:11). Although he was in his nineties, he was young in mind because of his prophetic outlook. His attitude contrasts radically with many Christians today who couldn't care less about this revelation. They spend countless hours reading newspapers and magazines, discussing current events and viewing TV programs but scarcely a single moment to read what the Lord predicts for the tomorrows!

The Lord tried to open the eyes of His generation but with little success. His censure of them is even more applicable to those living close to the end of this millennium:

> Ah, if you only knew, even at this eleventh hour, on what your peace depends—but you cannot see it. . . . (Luke 19:42 PHILLIPS)

... Yes, you know how to interpret the look of the sky but you have no idea how to interpret the signs of the times! (Matthew 16:3 PHILLIPS)

But John wept over the sealed scroll. Then one of the elders spoke, "Do not weep, the Lion of Judah will break the seals."

The elated John lifted his eyes to see this mighty lion, but no lion was visible. However, he was amazed at what he saw:

I looked and saw a Lamb standing there before the twenty-four elders, in front of the throne and the Living Beings, and on the Lamb were wounds that once had caused His death. . . . (5:6 LNT)

Not a powerful lion but a slain Lamb! Strange indeed that a slain Lamb could open this scroll that had thwarted everyone in the universe! John must have been dazed at such a spectacle!

Here is God sitting on His sapphire throne. Around Him is exquisite colorful beauty far beyond human words to paint: the impressive cherubim with their fiery whirling masses of color; the twenty-four Elders crowned and sitting on lovely thrones; and beyond these as far as the eye could see, in every direction, myriads and myriads of beautiful angels.

Yet, in this celestial setting, the very center of attention, is a slain Lamb with blood showing on its coat. It had been *killed* but surprisingly it *stands* endued with supreme power. This paradox the world has never understood.

This heavenly scene abounds with symbolism. In the Revelation, the characteristic title of our omnipotent Lord is the Lamb. It is used a total of twenty-nine times. Yet in all of the other books of the New Testament, this name is only applied to Christ four times. In those places the writers used the Greek word *amnos* for lamb. But in all of the twenty-nine times it is used in the Revelation, John always used the Greek *arnion,* which signifies a very young lamb, a lambkin. (See *Guide,* Appendix No.11.)

It seems that John used this special word for a very young lamb to emphasize the attitude of abject submission taken by our Lord. This strange title is frequently repeated to sharply focus on the attribute of our Lord that qualifies Him to open the scroll. In so doing, He gives every reader a pattern with which to shape his life

On the lamb were wounds that caused His death. These wounds were His credentials to open the scroll. Innumerable times the Christian has been told that his salvation is based on Jesus' death. But rarely,

34

if ever, has anyone told him that the book of His Revelation is an open book because He went all the way to Calvary.

What He has provided at such great cost, should certainly be scrutinized with reverential awe!

Observe that this Lamb that John saw is vastly different from any other lamb:

> . . . It had seven horns and seven eyes, which are the seven Spirits of God dispatched over the whole earth. (5:6 BERKELEY)

Seven horns. Horn is used many times in the Bible as a symbol of power. It is used of a nation (Daniel 8:3; Zechariah 1:18); of a king (Daniel 7:8,24; 8:5) and of a person (Job 16:15). *Seven* signifies infinite power.

Seven eyes, which are the seven Spirits of God dispatched over the whole earth. Seven eyes symbolize omniscience. The seven Spirits indicate His presence over the whole world and His ability to read the mind and heart of every individual. In this Lamb, despicable by earthly standards, reside the infinite power and understanding of all the members of the Trinity (See *Guide*, Appendix 12.)

John now sees the Lamb as He takes the scroll from His Father:

> . . . And the Lamb went up and took the scroll from the right hand of the One who sat on the throne. When He took it, the four living creatures and the twenty-four elders fell down before the Lamb. Each of the elders had a harp, and they held golden bowls full of incense, the prayers of God's people. . . . (5:7,8 NEB)

First to attest to the worthiness of the Lamb are the four Living Beings, most holy of God's creation. With them are the twenty-four Elders, representatives of the millions of redeemed saints. Each of these has a harp and a golden bowl of incense, holding the prayers of Christians still on the earth. These prayers ascend from the golden altar as a sweet savor to the Father on the throne (8:3,4). How precious, indeed, are the prayers of God's saints!

Previously the twenty-four Elders had sung the Oratorio of Creation in heaven (4:11). But now they sing a song that had never echoed in heaven—the Oratorio of Redemption.

> And they sing a new song, saying, "Thou art worthy to receive the book and to open its seals, because Thou wert

sacrificed and hast bought them for God with Thy blood, out
of every tribe and tongue and people and nation, and hast
made them royalty and priests for our God, and they shall
reign over the earth. (5:9,10 BERKELEY)

Thou art worthy to open its seals because Thou wert sacrificed. What
a statement! Worthy because Thou wert sacrificed! One cannot imagine any book costing such a price! Then why is the Book of Revelation
such a neglected book today? Strange! Here is a paradox that calls for
an explanation. Could unseen forces be conniving to keep Christians
from studying it?

*Thou hast bought them out of every tribe and tongue and people and
nation.* It is no coincidence that this four-pronged emphasis on universality occurs seven times in Revelation (5:9; 7:9; 10:11; 11:9; 13:7; 14:6;
17:15). What a grand and fitting climax to the universality of God's
love, first proclaimed in Genesis 12:3 and echoed throughout the
Word:

> And in thy seed [Christ] shall all the nations of the earth
> be blessed. . . . (Genesis 22:18 KJV. Also see Galatians 3:14–
> 16.)

> There is neither Jew nor Greek, there is neither bond nor
> free, there is neither male nor female: for ye are all one in
> Christ Jesus. (Galatians 3:28 KJV)

Since the Bible from Genesis to Revelation emphasizes that Jesus
Christ eliminates international boundaries, social and economic barri-
ers and distinctions of sex—all of which are currently causing the world
no end of trouble—wouldn't it be smart for Christians to *practice* God's
Word that they stoutly love. Much better than freezing it stiff in the
deep freeze! Incidentally, modern sociology must take a deep bow to
the Word of God which antedated their concepts by four thousand
years.

No sooner had the voices of the 24 Elders stopped when John heard
an angelic choir such as no mortal had ever heard:

> And I saw, and I heard the voice of many angels,
> who were in a circle round the throne and the living
> creatures and the elders; and their number was ten
> thousands of ten thousands and thousands of thousands;
> and they were saying with a great voice:

> The Lamb, which has been slain, is worthy to
> receive the power and the riches and the wisdom
> and the strength and the honour and the glory
> and the blessing. (5:11,12 BARCLAY)

John was nonplussed to express the number of the angels. Ten thousand is the largest unit in the Greek vocabulary: larger numbers are expressed in multiples of this unit. So John makes a plural out of it, multiplies it by itself and then adds thousands of thousands. Whether one counts angels, grains of sand or stars in the heaven, he quickly is overwhelmed by the infinite character of God's creation and the insignificance of man's mind.

How the aged and persecuted John must have revelled as he listened to that chorus of countless trillions of angels. The memory of these great musical numbers must have made future tribulations much more bearable to him—just as the anticipation of these should glorify every trial that comes our way.

Perhaps, because Paul saw and heard the glories of "the third heaven," he wrote:

> In my opinion whatever we may have to go through now is
> less than nothing compared with the magnificent future God
> has planned for us. (Romans 8:18 PHILLIPS)

Incidentally, Revelation 5 meets all the requirements of an oratorio: combination of solos and choruses with instruments, twenty-four harps in this case. Thus far in this oratorio, four parts have been given, all attesting to the worthiness of the Lamb to open this prophecy. From *Living New Testament*, consider these:

1 The solo of the mighty angel, "Who is worthy to open the scroll?"
2 The solo of the elder, "The Lion of the tribe of Judah has proved Himself worthy to open the scroll."
3 The song of the twenty-four elders with their harps, "Thou art worthy to open the scroll."
4 The chorus of innumerable angels, "The Lamb . . . is worthy to receive the power and the riches and the wisdom and the strength and the honor and the glory and the blessing."

Surely John did not need any further confirmation of the worthiness of the Lamb. But he received it:

Then I heard every created thing in heaven and on earth and under the earth and in the sea, all that is in them, crying:

"Praise and honor, glory and might, to Him who sits on the throne and to the Lamb for ever and ever!" (5:13 NEB)

Commenting on this verse Professor A.T. Robertson writes in *Word Pictures in the New Testament:*

> No created thing is left out. This universal chorus of praise to Christ from all created life reminds one of the profound mystical passage in Romans 8:20–22 concerning the sympathetic agony of creation. . . . If the trail of the serpent is on all creation, it will be ultimately thrown off.

Even animals are under the curse of sin. The law of the jungle prevails—stalking, killing, and eating one another. But Isaiah 11:6 harmonizes with Romans 8:20–22. Isaiah tells about that millennial day when the wolf shall dwell with the lamb, the leopard shall lie with the kid, along with the calf, the young lion and the fatling—while a little child shall lead them.

What a day that will be when all the animal creation will be gloriously delivered from all their miseries! What a chorus they will sing when they realize that by His death, Jesus has delivered them all.

What a thrill the Apostle John must have had when the Lord gave him a preview and a hearing aid to understand the entire animal creation sing their Hallelujah chorus! They all assented to the worthiness of the Lamb to open the book. John could understand the birds as they filled the air with their melodies of praise. For the first time he perceived the delight of the roosters as they gave their affirmation with a resounding *Cock-a doodle-do.* Every cricket chirped assent. Every cow mooed her approval while the lions roared their confirmations. I feel sure the elephants must have danced as they trumpeted their corroborations. And wouldn't I have liked to see the sight when every whale surfaced and shot high fountains of praise into the sky!

Here was a fulfillment of the Psalmist's request, "Let everything that hath breath praise the Lord . . ." (Psalm 150:6 KJV).

Finally, this Oratorio of Redemption was brought to a grand finale with a quartet composed of the four Living Beings, the cherubim, whose voices reverberate like the rolling thunder:

And the four Living Beings kept saying, "Amen!"
And the twenty-four elders fell down and worshiped Him.
(5:14 LP)

Reverential worship of God makes a fitting end to the glorious scenes and messages of the first five chapters of Revelation. Such worship sets a fine example for all of us to follow. With shoes off and head bowed, let us observe the worthy Lamb as He now breaks the first seal of prophetic utterances, especially tailored to *discern these times.*

5

UNITED NATIONS IN PROPHECY?

Revelation 6:1–4

Is the United Nations symbolized in prophecy? Everybody should have an informed answer to this question. These verses give pertinent clues.

> I further saw when the Lamb opened the first of the seven seals, and I heard one of the four living beings say with a voice like thunder, "Come!" Then I looked and saw a white horse, and its rider holding a bow. To him a crown was presented and he went out conquering and to conquer.
>
> And when He opened the second seal, I heard the second living being say, "Come!" Then another horse fiery red, went out, and its rider was empowered to take the peace away from the earth, so that people would butcher one another, and a huge sword was given him. (6:1–4 BERKELEY)

It is generally agreed that the red horse rider, equipped with a huge sword to take "the peace away from the earth," so that people "would butcher one another," is a great war. The color itself (red) symbolizes danger, bloodshed, and war. "From the earth" indicates the world-wide influence of these two riders.

Fiery red horse, empowered to take the peace away from the earth. What peace? The inference is that the red horse rider takes away *the peace* that the white horse rider had been trying to bring to the whole earth. White has for centuries been a symbol of peace.

Therefore, it seems logical to believe that the rider of the white horse is some organization seeking to bring *peace* to this earth. Nobody can disprove or prove this view. Time alone will give the correct answer. But every Christian scholar should keep this concept in mind as events of the future unroll.

Vividly I recall World War I and its slogan THIS IS A WAR TO END ALL WARS! When the war ended, the League of Nations was created "to achieve international *peace* and security." (Italics are mine.)

This League (1920–1946) had much in common with the rider on the white horse. Both were working for international peace. Both wore a crown symbolizing their authority to do this job. Both threatened to punish violators with a warlike bow. But the League and the white horse rider were helpless since neither had any arrows to enforce its decisions.

Former President Theodore Roosevelt said, "The League will fail because it has no teeth."

How did the League, brainchild of human idealism, succeed? In 1931 Japan took Manchuria. Bolivia and Paraguay were at war from 1932 to 1935. In 1933 Hitler withdrew from the League, rearmed, and seized Austria (1938). Mussolini attacked Ethiopia in 1935. That nation appealed to the League but received no help.

At Munich, in 1938, Britain and France appeased Hitler by carving out a piece of Czechoslovakia and throwing that to the German wolf. The League was thus wholly impotent when such powerful nations put national interests ahead of international justice!

Soon Hitler's mouth watered for Poland (1939). England and France had a treaty to protect Poland, but Hitler hesitated since he feared a Russian attack. Hitler then proposed a nonaggression pact to Russia. Previously Russia and Nazi Germany had been the bitterest of enemies. Yet Russia signed that pact and surprised the world. Why? A crafty Russia figured that if the European nations wore themselves down in a war, they would be an easy prey for the Russian bear.

On August 24, 1939, Hitler signed the nonaggression pact with Russia. Eight days later his panzers roared into Poland. Two days later England and France declared war against Germany. Before long many other nations were wallowing in a sea of blood as history's most awful war flooded the earth. And the League? What could an unarmed rider on a white horse do with such powerful nations on the warpath?

Just before World War II ended, forty-six war-weary nations met in San Francisco and organized the United Nations (June 26, 1945). The white horse which had been trotting around with the name of the *League of Nations* was now dripping with the blood of millions.

The League of Nations held its last meeting in Geneva. The members hosed off their white nag and shipped him to New York City. There his name was changed to United Nations. Then he was lavishly bedded in his luxurious glass barn on New York's East River.

But it was the same rider, the same horse, the identical crown, and the empty bow. His job was to keep the peace of the world.

The United Nations did have some measure of success when small nations were involved; regarding larger nations, let the record speak for itself.

The Communists took over Rumania in 1945, Hungary in 1948, and installed a pro-Soviet cabinet in Czechoslovakia in 1948. Supported by over 100 Russian-built tanks, North Korea invaded the Republic of Korea (South Korea) in 1950. The UN appealed for help, and naïve United States responded and carried the major load in the Korean War (1950–53), with the loss of thousands of men.

Space will not permit description of China's take-over of Tibet (1951), nor of Hungary's bid for freedom and her blood bath in 1956, nor of the slaughter in the Congo where Russia pulled the strings that worked her puppets. (Other reasons why the U.N. has not succeeded in keeping the peace are given in *Guide*, Appendix 14.)

In 1947 Russia hoped to use the Jews and Palestine as a launchpad to grab the oil-rich Middle East. Hence Russia voted in the UN to partition Palestine and make Israel an independent nation.

The UN voted that this partition, making Israel an independent nation, would begin May 14, 1948. On that day five Arab armies intent on killing every Israeli hurricaned through Israel. The Arab leaders would not abide by the world's duly constituted authority to give Israel a small piece of Palestine as a homeland. They defied not only the authority of man but the title deed of the country which God had given Israel (Genesis 15:18; 17:8; 48:4).

At the time of the invasion, the UN merely protested, but the Arabs scoffed at the hollow warnings from the arrowless world organization.

The greatly outnumbered Israeli knew that they were fighting for their lives. Desperately they fought; fervently they prayed! And the world was astounded when the newly born nation of Israel soundly trounced the five nations bent on her extermination.

Their miraculous victory can only be explained with one word— God! It was time on God's calendar for the valley of dry bones to come together (Ezekiel 37). It was time for the fig tree to send forth its leaves as the Lord Jesus predicted (Matthew 24:32–34).

But Israel had not suffered exile and slaughter for twenty-five hundred years to become a puppet of tyrannical and godless Russia. When the Soviet Union saw that she could not control Israel, she turned against the infant nation and has been seeking her scalp ever since.

Russia began to pour many millions of dollars into Egypt. Abetted by the Soviets, Egypt nationalized the Suez Canal (1956). With the wine of this steal in his head, Nasser began intolerable harassment of Israel. But Israel in a brilliant military campaign, aided by the British and French, quickly occupied the entire Sinai Peninsula (1956). When the United States pressured and assured Israel that her southern waterway, the Gulf of Aqaba, would be an international passage, Israel reluctantly pulled her army out of the Sinai Peninsula.

In 1967 tensions heightened quickly in the Middle East. Nasser demanded that UN Secretary General U Thant remove the UN emergency force interposed between Israel and Egypt. To the dismay of much of the world, U Thant immediately ordered every soldier to make a quick withdrawal. The white horse never made a whimper or a whine. With ears and tail flying straight back, it made a world-record getaway. At the one time when the white nag could have merited some of the millions of dollars of oats that it was consuming, it fled, just as Russia wanted it to do.

Next Nasser took Israel by the throat and tried to strangle her by closing the Gulf of Aqaba, the source of her oil and other supplies. Thus Nasser provoked the Six-Day War in June, 1967.

As Arabs poised to invade Israel, Nasser boasted, "If war breaks out it will be total in scope; the objective: annihilation of Israel. . . ." And the world feared it would be, since Russia had equipped and trained the Arab nations exceptionally well. But again the Arabs and the Soviets were wholly ignorant of God's calendar.

The war lasted only six days. In that short time Israel completely devastated the Arab armies and destroyed millions of dollars' worth of Soviet military hardware. The war can be described by one word: miraculous!

From the close of that war (June 1967) to the present, the Soviet Union has incited the Arab leaders to harass Israel with terror raids, artillery fire, and bombs. Yet with hundreds of observers from the UN around, I never once read of their putting the blame on the Arabs for initiating the artillery duels, the bombing of buses, or conducting murderous raids on peaceful farming communities. What is back of such chicanery? Communist Russia! All should read Raymond Carroll's informative article in the January 13, 1969, *Newsweek* titled, "The UN and Israel: 'The Deck is Stacked.' "

Another recent example of the UN's refusal to make even a verbal protest when the Soviet Union is involved has been disclosed by the Red Cross. In the November, 1968, *Reader's Digest* one reads the following taken from the book *Countdown in the Holy Land:*

The Soviet strategy of hiding behind proxies saved Russia from condemnation for an outrageous international crime. The fact is that in the Yemen war, Soviet bombers, maintained by Soviet mechanics and flown by Soviet-trained Egyptian pilots, repeatedly dropped Russian poison gas on Yemeni villages, killing and wounding several hundred civilians.

LESTER VELIE

The International Committee of the Red Cross delegation at Jidda, Saudi Arabia, responded to the call of the survivors. Although they gave the Egyptian authorities notice of the convoy's line of march and timetable, Egyptian pilots severely bombed the Red Cross convoys.

However, persistence on the part of the Red Cross finally won. When units did manage to reach the scene, some of the graves were opened. In one grave fifteen corpses were found. Autopsies by physicians left no doubt that death resulted from pulmonary edema, such as is seen in gas poisoning. Empty gas canisters with Russian markings were also found.

The Red Cross sent these findings to the proper authorities. *U.S. News and World Report* published them. From the *Reader's Digest* summary of Lester Velie's book, *Countdown in the Holy Land*, is this statement:

> Finally, pressed to speak out, Secretary-General U Thant said that everybody knew that he and the U.N. opposed poison gas, so why say anything about it? In any case, Cairo denied the charges; therefore it would be improper to take up the matter in the Security Council.

The duplicity of the white horse rider was seen in the disgraceful civilian slaughter and starvation of millions of Biafrans in Nigeria. There is also the continuing rape of the freedom of Czechoslovakia; yet the United Nations, duly crowned by 126 nations to correct these and other glaring injustices, stands helpless in the world's arena with empty words and an empty quiver.

Is the UN the white horse rider? Each must make his own conclusion after noting these significant similarities:

1 Both work for peace.
2 Both have a worldwide scope.
3 Both are crowned with authority to act.
4 Both have a threatening bow of bluff.
5 Both lack arrows to enforce its mandates.

What facts should one remember from this chapter? Four basic concepts should be stored in the mind.

1 The view that the white horse rider symbolizes the United Nations cannot be proved but it is a logical interpretation. (See *Guide*, appendixes 13 and 14.)
2 The godless Soviet Union controls the largest voting bloc in the United Nations.
3 Russia is dedicated to the destruction of Israel.
4 After the white horse rider, the Bible predicts the red horse rider—a war that will eclipse all previous wars.

This future war could come any day. Nobody can put a time tag on it. However, the Bible clearly outlines the events that follow this war. These will be studied in the next chapter.

6

NUCLEAR BOMBS ON GOD'S TIMETABLE?

Revelation 6:5–17

Most scholars agree that the red horse rider of the previous chapter is a huge war. Observe the sequelae of that war.

> When He [the Lamb] opened the third seal, I heard the third living being say, "Come!" Then I looked and saw a black horse, and its rider had a pair of scales in his hand. (6:5 BERKELEY)

Isn't it odd that the sole equipment of this rider is a pair of scales? To clinch the symbolism of the scales, John hears a supernatural voice from the center of the Living Beings. Since the throne of God is there, the voice must be that of God.

> I also heard something like a voice in the center of the four living beings, that said, "A quart of wheat for a day's wage and

three quarts of barley for a day's wage, and do not damage the
oil and the wine. (6:6 BERKELEY)

A measure of wheat (KJV) for a day's wage. Scholars believe that this
measure, less than a quart, would be needed to keep one man alive.
If a man earned $25 a day, it would mean that he would have to spend
the entire amount for a quart of wheat. At that price a bushel of wheat
would sell for $800. Proportioned to the current ratio (price of wheat
to price of bread), a loaf of bread would cost $180.

Three measures (KJV) of barley for a day's wage. If a man had a small
family, his entire wage would be needed to buy the cheaper barley for
them. Of course, there would be nothing left for housing, clothes, heat,
medicine, and dozens of other needed items. The Lord is telling John
that after this great war there will be a famine of almost unbelievable
severity.

Our world has experienced two world wars. In both of these, prices
jumped. But those increases are insignificant compared to the prices
in this future war.

In the past commentators were at a loss to explain a famine of such
gravity, but since the discovery of atomic and hydrogen bombs, people
realize that this prediction is not only possible but very likely.

The bomb used at Hiroshima was equivalent to twenty kilotons,
20,000 tons of the powerful explosive TNT. The heat of that explosion
gave third degree burns and started fires in a circle two miles in
diameter. The terrific heat, the devastation, and the slaughter that it
produced dumbfounded the world.

Yet, compared to the bombs today, that bomb is dubbed a fire-
cracker. In fact, bombs are not rated anymore by the thousands of tons
but by the *millions of tons*—megatons. Experts give the potential of
these bombs:

> According to one estimate, one-10 megaton bomb
> could spread searing heat over 5,000 square
> miles, which is about the area of the state of
> Connecticut.

> According to one set of calculations, a 1,000-
> megaton bomb detonated at satellite altitude
> could set six Western states afire.
> THE FALLEN SKY

These bombs are exploded at high altitudes to obtain a wider cone
of coverage. At high altitudes the atmosphere is so rarefied that there

is little loss of heat energy. Such bombs would readily destroy all grain, livestock, and people over huge areas. Perhaps the Biblical predictions of extreme famine conditions did seem absurd to readers a few decades ago. But not today!

Do not damage the oil and the wine. Do not destroy the olive trees and the grape vines. Only comparatively small bombs able to destroy grains are permitted. Prohibited are those that could destroy the hardy vines and trees. The greater hardiness of trees over grains is also brought out in a later war when more powerful weapons are used. Of this war one reads, ". . . the third part of trees was burnt up and all green grass was burnt up . . ." (8:7 KJV).

It is important to note that in this war, the vegetation is destroyed by *heat.*

Do not damage the oil and the wine. Here and elsewhere one is reminded that everything is under God's control (Rev.6:1,3,5,7,12; 8:1,2,7,8,10,12; 9:1,13). Not a hand can be raised, not a wheel can turn until He permits. Those Christians who will be exposed to the hatred of the Antichrist (13:7,15–17) should ever remember and draw encouragement from this fact.

The last of the four horsemen is the most frightening:

> When He opened the fourth seal, I heard the voice of the fourth Living Being say, "Come!" (6:7 BERKELEY)
> Again I looked and there appeared a horse sickly green in color. The name of its rider was death, and the grave followed close behind him. . . . (6:8 PHILLIPS)
> . . . And power was given unto them over the fourth part of the earth, to kill with sword, and with hunger, and with death and with the beasts of the earth. (6:8 KJV)

The name of this rider is Death or Pestilence and his inseparable companion is the Grave. Both seem to be seated on one horse. (See *Guide,* appendix 15.)

Power over the fourth part of the earth to kill. Of course, the slaughter is confined to those nations at war. Quite a few nations would be involved if a fourth of the earth's surface is affected. If one fourth of the earth's population is in view here, then it would mean the death of 850 million. Military experts state that if the United States engages in a war with a nuclear power, that 90% of the people would die. That means the death of 181 million Americans. If the nations of Europe and Asia with their many hundreds of millions are also in it, a total mortality of 850 million is easy to understand.

In World War I the deaths on all sides totaled 10 million. The World War II figures range between 20 and 50 million. But the future war will snuff out 850 million. The frightening difference indicates something similar to a nuclear war.

What percentage of this astronomical total will be civilian deaths? In World War I only 5 percent of the deaths were civilian. In World War II the percentage jumped to 48 percent. In the Korean war it was 84 percent, while the estimate for Vietnam runs about 90 percent according to an article by Donald T. Kauffman appearing in August, 1969, *Christian Herald*.

Let's face it, in view of the extreme vulnerability of the civilian population to nuclear attack, the civilian percentage in the future wars could well be in the high 90s.

In 1962 I attended a New York State medico-military conference. The emphasis was on the construction of basement shelters, on fallout, and the need of giving twenty-five blood transfusions to those moderately far removed from the explosion.

But in 1970 one does not put the emphasis on such matters. With bombs measured by the millions of tons of TNT exploded high in the air, the problem is not fallout but the terrific unbelievable heat produced by the bomb. Ordinary basement shelters might protect from moderate fallout but not from the intense heat measured by millions of degrees. "Within the incendiary radius of a big bomb, however, the basement shelter becomes a firetrap," according to Gerard Piel in *The Fallen Sky*.

A 100-megaton bomb would produce so much heat that everything combustible within a circle 140 miles in diameter would immediately burst into flames. Add to that intense heat, the heat caused by the burning, at the same time, of all the houses in a metropolitan area. Add to that the burning of all vegetation and trees in a circle 140 miles in diameter. Then add to that inconceivable conflagration the fire-storm winds measured by the hundreds of miles an hour velocity. Yes, the result is utterly unthinkable!

One can understand how millions will die from the direct effect of blast, heat, and fallout. When the war is over the rider on the black horse will ride out on a barren blackened landscape with a pair of scales in his hand. With bread selling for $180 a loaf countless millions more will die of famine and the ensuing pestilences.

Kill with sword, with hunger, with pestilences and with the beasts. What beast? Most of the carnivora would die from the bombs or from starvation. Could it be insects who are very resistant to high-energy radiation? Insects would multiply readily with their enemies the birds

47

dead. These insects could "quickly destroy every green thing left by fire and bomb," declares Bentley Glass in *The Fallen Sky*.

Killed with beasts. I doubt if carnivora or insects are in view here. In Greek the word for beast is *therion*. This word is used here and thirty-seven other times in Revelation. In all of these thirty-seven times, the word consistently refers to the beastly Antichrist or his False Prophet. Since these two wicked men are called *beast* thirty-seven times, is it not logical to believe that these wicked men are in view in the thirty-eighth occurrence of the word?

And especially so since repeated mention is made in Revelation of their murderous activities (7:9–14; 11:7–10; 12:1–17; 13:1–17). In fact, the number killed by these two beastly men will be so large "which no man could number" (7:9 KJV). (Also see *Guide*, Appendix 16.)

Confirmation that these two human "beasts" are the murderous agents is supported by the verses which immediately follow Revelation 6:8:

> When the Lamb broke the fifth seal, I could see, beneath the altar, the souls of those who had been killed for the sake of the Word of God and because of the faithfulness of their witness. They cried out in a loud voice, saying,
> "How long shall it be, O Lord of all, holy and true, before Thou shalt judge and avenge our blood upon the inhabitants of the earth?"
> Then each of them was given a white robe, and they were told to be patient a little longer, until the number of their fellow servants and of their brethren, who were to die as they had died, should be complete. (6:9–11 PHILLIPS)

These Christians will be martyred because they read God's Word and witness to His goodness. Obeying the Lord will be their only crime.

This great tribulation is described immediately after the terrible war, famine, and pestilence. It appears, therefore, that the victor in this war is a godless nation, possessed by a Satanic spirit to eradicate Christianity from the earth. Not only here but other writers stress that this anti-Christ spirit is one of the identifying signs of His return (Matthew 24:9–13; 2 Thessalonians 2:3; 2 Timothy 3:1; 2 Peter 3:3).

Could any nation in this century be tailored to take such an anti-Christ stance? Russia and its refractory child, China, are completely dedicated to wipe away every trace of God, not alone within their own borders, but from the whole earth. And their success has been spectacular in Europe, Asia, Africa, and South America. Particularly frightening in England and the United States is the extensive infiltration of godless ideologies—sexual promiscuity, lawlessness, terrorism, and destruction of every vestige of Christian society.

While the United States slept under a Satanic trance, Russia established her puppet Castro in Cuba. And on that island in our own front yard are probably missile bases that could level every important city in the eastern half of the United States!

Within the United States itself are at least half a dozen well-organized, well-trained, and dedicated groups who publicly and repeatedly boast that they will destroy the Establishment. That includes Christianity. They blatantly assert that they will not hesitate to kill everybody who stands in their way.

And they have given plenty illustrations of their power to tie up in knots the greatest Christian nation on earth. These powerful godless groups have ballooned their numbers by pretending interest in a variety of minority groups on the basis of war, poverty, and race. They attract others by advocating sexual promiscuity, nudity and freedom to "do their thing, anytime, anywhere, regardless of circumstances."

When the members of these groups become addicted to drugs they will commit any crime to get a fix.

Since it is widely believed and has been proved that some of the leaders of these godless groups are Communists, one can see how difficult it would be for the United States to win in a war with Russia as the foe. Sabotage, refusal to be drafted, and widespread violence could cripple the entire war effort.

This has been the pattern of Soviet take-over. One should not say, "It can't happen in the United States." It is happening! In fact, it has advanced so far that there is only one hope for this country—a spiritual revival. God could and would save us if the people who are called by His name would humble themselves, pray, and turn from their wicked ways (2 Chronicles 7:14). And there is help in no other course.

How long, O Lord, . . . before Thou shalt . . . avenge our blood? With all hats off to the enviable fidelity of these martyrs under the altar, yet their prayers are sadly different from those of Jesus and Stephen, who when dying prayed for their tormentors. Furthermore, they could not understand why God was so slow to avenge their death.

They are like many wonderful Christians today who would die for their faith in God's Word, but who are pathetically ignorant of God's timetable of the events that precede His return to this earth.

49

A few days before Jesus was crucified, His disciples asked Him for that timetable. He then gave them the signs—the events that would occur just before He returned (Matthew 24).

The timetable that Jesus gave to His disciples in Matthew 24 is the same and in the same order that Jesus revealed when He opened the six seals in Revelation 6.

To *discern these times* no study of Scripture is more important than a comparison of chapter 6 of Revelation and 24 of Matthew.

1. The Prince of Peace stated that mimicking Christs would first come (Matthew 24:5). How similar to Revelation 6:1,2—the white horse rider, the mimic who promises peace by human means, the United Nations.
2. Jesus told about wars (Matthew 24:6). And the facsimile of this prediction is the rider on the red horse who wields a huge sword (Revelation 6:4).
3. Next the Lord warned about ensuing famine (Matthew 24:7)— the equivalent of the third seal, the rider with a pair of scales (Revelation 6:5,6).
4. Jesus predicted deadly pestilences (Matthew 24:7; Luke 21:11), the same as the sickly green horse rider who is called by different translators as Pestilence or Death (Revelation 6:8).
5. Our Lord next predicted the Great Tribulation, "when men will hand you over to persecution, and kill you" (Matthew 24:9 PHILLIPS; 24:21). The counterpart of this is the fifth seal, the view of the martyrs under the altar (Revelation 6:9; 7:9,14).
6. To His disciples Jesus said, ". . . immediately after the tribulation of those days shall the sun be darkened, and the moon shall not give her light, and the stars shall fall from heaven . . ." (Matthew 24:29 ASV). Compare this with the day of God's wrath: ". . . the sun black as sackcloth of hair, and the moon became as blood; and the stars of heaven fell unto the earth . . ." (Revelation 6:12,13 KJV).

This comparison of Matthew 24 and Revelation 6 is another example of the remarkable unity of the Bible—a solid proof of its inspiration.

When *informed* Christians, living during the tribulation, see the events described in the first five seals transpire, their faith in their Lord's predictions will be strengthened. Thus, they will be greatly encouraged to remain faithful and to resist the pressures of the Antichrist. To be forewarned is to be forearmed! (See *Guide*, Appendix 17.)

How long, O Lord? These martyrs never knew or had failed to remember that the prophets Daniel and John repeatedly stated that the Great Tribulation will last 3½ years (Daniel 7:25; 9:27; 12:7; Revelation 11:3; 12:6,14; 13:5).

One may wonder why the Lord permits the Antichrist to persecute and martyr Christians for 3½ years. Back of this long waiting period is the fathomless love of God. Before His awful wrath falls in the sixth seal, He uses extreme measures to save the wicked from their eternal fate (2 Peter 3:9; Revelation 8:13; 11:3; 14:6,7; 16:15; 18:4).

When the Lamb opens the sixth seal, the time for repentance is over:

> Then I watched while He broke the sixth seal. There was a tremendous earthquake, the sun turned dark like a coarse black cloth, and the full moon was red as blood. The stars of the sky fell upon the earth, just as a fig tree sheds unripe figs when shaken in a gale. The sky vanished as though it were a scroll being rolled up, and every mountain and island was jolted out of its place. Then the kings of the earth, and the great men, the captains, the wealthy, the powerful, and every man, whether slave or free, hid themselves in caves and among mountain rocks. They called out to the mountains and the rocks:
> "Fall down upon us and hide us from the face of him who sits upon the throne, and from the wrath of the Lamb! For the great day of their wrath has come, and who can stand against it?" (Revelation 6:12–17 PHILLIPS)

This great day of God's wrath is so important that a special chapter will be given to it. All Christians both dead and living will be caught up to be with their Lord before that most terrible of all days comes (John 5:24–29). This is the day of God's judgment on the wicked. It must not be confused with the Great Tribulation as some people do. There is no excuse for this error as Jesus explicitly stated that "immediately after the tribulation" this day of divine judgment will occur (Matthew 24:29 KJV).

Now to summarize Revelation 6. It begins with the white horse rider which could well be the United Nations. The chapter then predicts a future war to be followed by an awful famine and deadly pestilences. Then one sees the souls who have been martyred in the Great Tribulation. The chapter closes with the return of the Lord to pour out His wrath on a wicked world.

51

7

COURAGE FOR THE CRISIS

Revelation 7

One had a glimpse of the Christian martyrs when the fifth seal was opened. John will give much more detail about this Great Tribulation later. The Lord first gives three scenes to cheer His followers during this awful ordeal. Here is the first scene:

> Following this, I saw four angels stationed at the four corners of the earth, restraining the four winds of the earth, so that no wind might blow on land or sea or on any tree. I also observed another angel ascending from the sunrise, holding a seal from the living God. He shouted with a loud voice to the four angels, who had been empowered to injure the earth and the sea. (7:1,2 BERKELEY)

Here as in Revelation 6 the activities of wicked men are all under God's control. They can do nothing unless the Lord permits.

Repeated mention is made in chapters 7 and 8 of injury to earth, sea, and trees. How could any war injure earth, sea, and trees? In the past commentators could not answer that one. But now even small youngsters are aware of the destructive power of napalm, nuclear, and other deadly agents to spoil earth, sea, and trees.

When will this devastation occur? In the unit comprised of the first four seals, the destruction of olive trees was forbidden by God (6:6). Therefore, it seems that the blowing of the trumpets must occur *after* the fourth seal. And it must occur *before* the sixth seal, the terminal event of this age.

Therefore, it seems logical to believe that the trumpets blow during the fifth seal.

But before the first trumpet blows, one of God's great angels gives a restraining order to the wicked destroyers.

> "Wait! Don't do anything yet—hurt neither earth nor sea nor trees—until we have placed the Seal of God upon the foreheads of His servants."

How many were given this mark? I heard the number—it was 144,000, out of all the twelve tribes of Israel as listed here:

Judah	12,000
Reuben	12,000
Gad	12,000
Asher	12,000
Naphtali	12,000
Manasseh	12,000
Simeon	12,000
Levi	12,000
Issachar	12,000
Zebulun	12,000
Joseph	12,000
Benjamin	12,000

(7:3–8 LNT)

A unique repetition! Why? The Lord wanted to clinch the concept that this group was composed of Israelites. He could have stated that there were 144,000 Israelites. But, no! He does it emphatically, detailing the twelve tribes by name and specifying that each tribe had 12,000. He wants to focus attention on the symbolic significance of the number twelve, the symbolical designation of Israel. (See *Guide*, Appendix 18 for explanation).

In spite of this clear identification, some state that this group represents the church. But they forget that Revelation 1:20 clearly states that the lampstands are the symbols of the churches. (A fuller explanation of the 144,000 Israelites will be taken up in later chapters, but an informative summary of this group in Scripture is given in *Guide*, Appendix 19.)

Furthermore, to think of the 144,000 Israelites as the church is illogical, since the next scene clearly visualizes an innumerable number of Christians.

After this I saw a vast crowd, too great to count, from all nations and provinces and languages, standing in front of the throne and before the Lamb, clothed in white, with palm branches in their hands.

And they were shouting with a mighty shout, "Salvation comes from our God upon the throne, and from the Lamb." (7:9,10 LNT)

This group is not only Christian but they present three other contrasts to the 144,000 Israelites because they are multiracial, innumerable, and are in heaven.

Robed in white. White is one of the great adjectives of the Revelation, occurring as it does almost twice as often in this book as in all the rest of the New Testament. In Revelation it is always used in a symbolic sense to denote purity or peace. The church at Sardis was told how to obtain the white robe, "He that overcometh, the same shall be clothed in white raiment . . ." (3:5 KJV).

They had palms in their hands. Only here and at the triumphal entry is mention made of waving palm branches, a symbol of adoration and rejoicing.

Rejoicing along with this vast number of tribulation Christians were countless millions of angels:

> And now all the angels were crowding around the throne and around the elders and the four Living Beings, and falling face down before the throne and worshiping God.
>
> "Amen!" they said. "Blessing, and glory, and wisdom, and thanksgiving, and honor, and power, and might be to our God forever and forever. Amen!" (7:11,12 LNT)

The seven words of angelic adoration used here are the same as those used in Revelation 5:11,12, with one exception: *Thanksgiving* is fittingly used here in place of *riches,* as an expression of gratitude for divine help given to these Christians in the Tribulation.

> Then one of the twenty-four elders asked me, "Do you know who these are, who are clothed in white, and where they come from?"
>
> "No, sir," I replied. "Please tell me."
>
> "These are the ones coming out of the Great Tribulation," he said; "they washed their robes and whitened them by the blood of the Lamb. (7:13,14 LNT)

These are the ones coming out of the Great Tribulation. The tense of the verb indicates that the martyrs are still arriving from the scene of the great tribulation. Likewise, when John saw the same souls of the martyrs under the altar, their number was still increasing (6:11). In both scenes the Great Tribulation was still in progress. Incidentally, a comparison of these two scenes indicates that the time of the fifth seal is the same as that of the Great Tribulation, as previously stated.

A vast crowd, too great to count. It is thrilling to note that in spite of the persecution, the sexual rottennesses of that day and the wide-

54

spread apostasy of the church, yet an innumerable number of Christians will be more than conquerors. Impossible? ". . . God is faithful, who will not suffer you to be tempted above that ye are able . . ." (1 Corinthians 10:13 KJV).

All of us would prefer to think that no Christian will suffer at the time of the Great Tribulation. But these verses and those in Revelation 6:9–11; 12:17; 13:7 and elsewhere give unmistakable evidence that Christians will suffer in the Great Tribulation. Of course, no Christian will suffer *any* of the much greater miseries of the day of God's Wrath, as will be shown later in detail in chapter 24.

However, this view of millions singing God's praises after passing through the Tribulation proves what the Apostle Paul exultingly affirmed, "For I reckon that the sufferings of this present time are not worthy to be compared with the glory which shall be revealed in us" (Romans 8:18 KJV).

Observe how the Lord rewards His faithful followers:

> . . . they have washed their robes and have made them white in the blood of the Lamb. For this reason they are before God's throne, and day and night serve Him in His temple, while He Who sits on the throne spreads His tent over them. They shall nevermore either hunger or thirst, nor shall the sun or any heat whatever beat upon them; for the Lamb, Who has ascended the center of the throne, shall shepherd them and shall lead them them to springs of living water. And God shall wipe away all tears from their eyes. (Revelation 7:14–17 BERKELEY)

They shall nevermore hunger. When the third seal was opened, a whole day's wage was required to buy a few handfuls of grain (6:5,6). Then when the first trumpet blows, a third of all the trees and all the grass with its grain will be destroyed (8:7). These are not alone the predictions of God's Word but the probabilities of the tomorrows as expressed by well-informed scientists of this century.

Add to these unthinkable famine conditions the restrictions imposed by the Antichrist on Christians buying or selling anything unless they give up their faith and receive his mark. The believers living during the Great Tribulation will be sorely pressed to obtain anything to eat. But they must ever remind themselves that the time will soon come when hunger will be a faint memory of the past.

Neither thirst. Today that doesn't seem much of a promise! But to those living at the time of the Tribulation, this will be a most precious promise. Of this period one reads, ". . . men in great numbers died of the water because it had been poisoned" (8:11 NEB). If one drinks such water contaminated by fallout or bacteria or chemicals, he could die a painful cholera-type death. Knowing this fact, people will endure the miseries of extreme dehydration.

Nor shall the sun or any heat whatever beat upon them. One can't detail the source of these unusual sun rays and extreme heat. Perhaps, the thermal effects of nuclear bombs may be in view, or one of the newer weapons that the geophysicists are feverishly working on! They are currently seeking practical ways to blow holes in the ozone layer above the atmosphere. This ozone layer protects all forms of life from the deadly ultraviolet rays of the sun. To blow a hole in this layer over an enemy country would be to destroy all life in that country.

And God shall wipe all tears from their eyes. Looking ahead to that day, believers will be much better able to suffer hunger, thirst, and burning rays from the sun—yes, with much greater grace and fortitude than those in the world. They will know that all of these horrors were predicted by God and this knowledge will give them better grace to endure the trials of that period. And this preview of the shouting overcomers should hearten every suffering saint!

Just before the first trumpet sounds, the Lord reveals the third and last scene intended to give courage for the awful impending crisis:

> Also another angel with a golden censer came and took his stand at the altar. A vast quantity of incense was given him, so that he might place it with the prayers of all the saints on the golden altar before the throne. And the smoke of the incense arose from the angel's hand with the prayers of the saints before God. (8:3,4 BERKELEY)

Another angel (aggelos). Aggelos can just as well be translated as a divine agent. Hence, Dr. John F. Walvoord states in *The Revelation of Jesus Christ* that "the preponderance of opinion seems to favor regarding the angel as Christ." (See *Guide,* Appendix 20 for further light on this subject.)

Personally, I am greatly moved to think of our Lord, our heavenly High Priest and Intercessor, taking our stuttered phrases and mixing them with "a vast quantity of incense" distilled in Gethsemane and Golgotha. How much our human, our earthly centered petitions need to be mixed with His incense, His own Spirit! The prayers of a tortured saint need the same fragrance of Him who gasped, "Father, forgive them for they know not what they do."

How consoling to remember that our prayers, mixed with His burning incense, arises as a fragrant perfume to our Father on the throne!

The golden censer . . . the golden altar. This costly metal symbolizes the high esteem with which God considers the prayers of His children. Today this thought is encouraging to every Christian, but it will be doubly so to those Christians suffering the torments of the Great Tribulation.

The first scene, that of the sealing of the 144,000 Israelites, purports to encourage and give direction to those Israeli who take the Lord's plan of escape (Matthew 24:21). The second scene gives encouragement by depicting the eternal rewards of the overcomers. The third scene shows the efficacy of prayers made in His name.

All three scenes give courage for the impending crisis—the Great Tribulation. This momentous period will be portrayed in the next chapter.

8

THE TIME OF SATAN'S WRATH

Revelation 8

The Apostle John wept when he first saw the scroll of the Revelation sealed with seven seals. But not for long—after the Lamb of God stepped forth. When He broke six of these seals, John saw the remarkable prophecies described in Revelation 6.

When the Lamb broke the seventh or last seal, then all the rest of the scroll could be unrolled, thus giving us the remaining chapters of Revelation. Observe the first of these glorious scenes:

> When the Lamb had broken the seventh seal, there was silence throughout all heaven for what seemed like half an hour.
> And I saw the seven angels that stand before God and they were given seven trumpets. (8:1,2 LNT)

Silence in heaven. Why? This holy hush may reflect the deep concern of those in heaven for the people on earth who will experience terrible distress when the trumpets sound. Perhaps everything in heaven is stilled to symbolize the priority that God gives to the faintest heart cry of His persecuted children. The next verses lend credence to this viewpoint:

> Then another angel with a golden censer came and stood at the altar; and a great quantity of incense was given to him to mix with the prayers of God's people, to offer upon the golden altar before the throne.
> And the perfume of the incense mixed with prayers ascended up to God from the altar where the angel had poured them out. (8:3,4 LNT)

The same angel who graciously added large amounts of incense to the prayers of the persecuted saints, now takes a totally different attitude toward their tormentors.

> Then the angel filled the censer with fire from the altar and threw it down upon the earth; and thunder crashed and rumbled, lightning flashed, and there was a terrible earthquake. (8:5 LNT)

Thunder, lightning, and earthquake—symbols of God's wrath—portray His attitude toward the wicked persecutors. These are signs that God is not only alive but that He will soon punish them for their evil deeds. This punishment, double for all their sins, will be described in a later chapter.

> Then the seven angels with the seven trumpets prepared to blow their mighty blasts.
> The first angel blew his trumpet, and hail and fire mixed with blood were thrown down upon the earth. *One-third* of the earth was set on fire so that *one-third* of the trees were burned, and all the green grass. (8:6,7 LNT)

(The italics *one-third* here and in later verses are mine.)

The first angel blew his trumpet. The Lord wanted Israel to blow silver trumpets for several occasions (Numbers 10:10). Very often they were blown as an alarm of impending danger (Exodus 19:19–21; Numbers 10:5–9; 2 Chronicles 13:12; Jeremiah 4:19; Joel 2:1; Zephaniah 1:16). In Revelation the trumpet sound symbolizes the Lord's voice and is blown to alert and protect from coming calamities.

Hence, the first six trumpets are divine signs of danger to His people. But the ensuing happenings are works of Satan. These Satanic events should never be called "judgments." By definition a judgment is "a calamity sent by God as a punishment." The Apostle John *never* uses the word *judgment* to refer to the events under the trumpets.

Therefore, it is most significant that John does use the words *judgment* and *judge* fourteen times to refer to the wrath of God, as in the pouring out of the bowls of wrath (chapters 15 and 16).

The exciting parallelism of bowls and trumpets in having common targets will be shown later. Clearly it is God who dispenses wrath under the bowls, but under the trumpets it is Satan who is the murderous activist. God and Satan are the two antagonists who seem to use nations favorable to their aims. The Satanic venom of the trumpets seems to be directed primarily against Israel, whereas the first six bowls seem to have as their target the Antichrist and his kingdom (Revelation 16:2,6,10,12). Christians are warned to flee from such territory (18:4). Before the seventh bowl, the great day of God's wrath, Christ will catch away His bride to be with Him. The church will not experience the awful day of God's wrath. This great day is fully described in chapter 24.

To understand the sequence of the great events in the tomorrows, one should study carefully the following chart on the chronology of Revelation:

CHRONOLOGY OF THE BOOK OF REVELATION

	United Nations ?	A Great War, Famine, and Death	The Great Tribulation	LORD'S	Day of God's Wrath on All Wicked	THE MILLENNIUM, Rev. 20:4	REVOLT OF SATAN	NEW HEAVEN & EARTH, Rev. 21 & 22
Seals	1	2-3-4	Satan's Wrath 5th Seal	RETURN	6th Seal			
Trumpets			Main target Israel 1-2-3-4-5-6	Matt. 24: 29-31	Last or 7th Trumpet			
Bowls of God's Wrath			God's Wrath on Kingdom of Antichrist 1-2-3-4-5-6	1 Cor. 15:52 Rev. 10:7	7th Bowl			

One-third of the earth was set on fire (8:7). This is the first of fourteen occurrences of the fraction one-third. This fraction is found nowhere else in the New Testament. Its bizarre repetitious use is confined entirely to Satan and his activities under the trumpets. What is the significance of such strange repetitiveness? Just as the number 7 symbolizes God's omnipotence, omniscience, and omnipresence, the fraction one-third symbolizes Satan and his finite power. "One-third of the earth" is a lot in human eyes but inconsequential compared to the multiplied trillions of heavenly bodies that God controls.

One third of the trees were burned and all the green grass. Here is something new—destruction of trees—not previously permitted in the unit of the first four seals (6:6). Comparison of 6:6 with 8:7 indicates that the first trumpet must begin after the fourth seal, as shown on the chart.

One third of the trees . . . all the green grass. Such devastation was ridiculed before the first atomic bomb (1945). Today with the more powerful nuclear bombs, such destruction is feared and thought probable in the days ahead. Observe that this verse states that the earth, the trees, and the grass are to be *burned.* In its prediction of *widespread thermal devastation* the Bible was ahead of modern military tactics by nineteen hundred years!

> Then the second angel blew his trumpet, and what appeared to be a huge burning mountain was thrown into the sea, destroying *a third* of all the ships; and a *third* of the sea turned red as blood; and *a third* of the fish were killed. (8:8,9 LNT)

When a test bomb was dropped at Bikini, Major Swancutt reported in *Atomic Bomb* by H.W. Gretzinger: "I saw a solid ball of fire fifteen miles in diameter cover the entire target area over the lagoon."

How similar to the falling "huge burning mountain"!

A third of the living creatures in the sea dies (Weymouth). That is not hard to believe after noting the destruction and poisoning of marine life when a comparatively small bomb was dropped over Bikini in 1946. But it is difficult to imagine the killing power of the bombs now. From the December 8, 1944, issue of *Christianity Today* comes this observation:

> In the 50 plus megaton range, 2500 times greater than what leveled Hiroshima and Nagasaki, the bomb was equal in explosive power to a train of TNT-loaded boxcars extending from New York to Los Angeles.

One can excuse Princeton Theological Seminary Professor Charles Erdman, writing nine years before atomic bombs, as he gives his opinion of the trumpets in Revelation in his exposition *The Revelation of John:*

> To regard the descriptions as literal predictions of actual catastrophies . . . would lead one into the sphere of the fanciful or the grotesque.

But now Wheaton's Merrill C. Tenny sees that atomic weapons can produce the physical cataclysms without divine intervention, as he states in *Interpreting Revelation.* Dallas Theological Seminary President John Walvoord writes in his study of Revelation, "There is no solid reason for not taking these catastrophies in a literal sense."

The first atomic bomb was exploded July 16, 1945. Compared to the mighty giants of today this bomb was a premature infant. Yet this infant generated 100 million degrees of heat. The steel tower made of heavy railroad rails was vaporized. The explosion made a hole in the ground six feet deep and five thousand feet wide. The heat was felt one hundred miles in all directions.

Of Hiroshima one reads that the people on the street exposed to the direct rays of the white heat above them fell in their tracks, their flesh scorched and bleeding at every wound.

And there came hail. When the bomb exploded at Bikini, "ten millions tons of water were tossed up in the sky as a result of the explosion of less than half the weight of an American dime in explosive material," writes Harold Gretzinger in *Christian Life.* Because of the terrific heat the water was vaporized and carried several miles high where the sub-zero temperature froze it into hailstones weighing hundreds of pounds. Dents on the tops of some of the experimental vessels were thought by some to be caused by the fall of these huge hailstones although this explanation may not be the correct one.

Neither can one tell whether this burning mountainous mass will be a nuclear device, burning napalm, or something yet to be discovered. Whatever it will be, it will have the aura of the miraculous to the unsophisticated. In fact, the Bible predicts that the Satanically controlled Antichrist will create widespread fear by using apparent supernatural phenomenon:

> He did unbelievable miracles such as making fire flame down to earth from the skies while everybody was watching. (13:13 LNT)

It is thrilling to me that John predicted such an unbelievable miracle in his century that was not possible until our century.
How can one explain the havoc produced by the third trumpet?

> The third angel blew, and a great flaming star fell from heaven upon a third of the rivers and springs.
> The star was called "Bitterness" because it poisoned a third of all the waters on the earth and many people died. (8:10,11 LNT)

Stars are used in Scripture as symbols of both good and evil beings (Genesis 37:9-11; Numbers 24:17; Isaiah 14:12 ASV; 2 Peter 1:19; Revelation 1:20; 9:1; 12:1,4; 22:16).

The star poisoned the water and many people died. This to the people in the first century was another unbelievable miracle. Such widespread poisoning of water was not possible until this day. Now such a feat is possible with several modern agents: germs, poisons, and radiation fallout, to mention a few. If one wants to take a look at the frightening arsenal of such weapons, then read a book written by more than a dozen distinguished scientists—*Unless Peace Comes* by Nigel Calder and others.

To some who have not kept abreast with the latest scientific discoveries, the prediction of the fourth trumpet will certainly seem to be humanly impossible:

> The fourth angel blew his trumpet and immediately *a third* of the sun was blighted and darkened, and a third of the moon and the stars, so that daylight was dimmed by *a third,* and the nighttime darkness deepened. (8:12 LNT)

Professor MacDonald, Associate Director of the Institute of Geophysics and Planetary Physics at UCLA, writes on the subject "How to Wreck the Environment." He states that even today scientists know that the introduction of certain materials into the upper atmosphere can produce changes that would darken the light of the sun, moon, and stars. Military researchers are seeking to perfect this principle. Ability to darken the sky would have tremendous military and psychological value.

> As I watched, I saw a solitary eagle flying through the heavens crying loudly, "Woe, woe, woe to the people of the earth because of the terrible things that will soon happen when the three remaining angels blow their trumpets." (8:13 LNT)

> The fifth angel blew his trumpet; and I saw a Star which had fallen from heaven to the earth; and to him was given the key . . . of the bottomless pit. (9:1 WEYMOUTH)

Star which had fallen. The only record of "a star which had fallen" is the star of the third trumpet (8:10). Scholars such as Swete and Louis Talbot believe that the star of the third and fifth trumpet is the same. (See *Guide,* Appendix 21 for summary on Satan.)

What being is so important as to claim the center of the stage in two trumpets? Certain facts point to Satan. Observe that a *woe* is pronounced on the people of the earth (8:13) when the star of Revelation 9:1 falls on the earth. Significantly, in Revelation 12:9,12 where Satan is definitely identified, a *woe* is also pronounced on the people of the earth when he falls down upon the earth.

Because of this close association, outstanding scholars believe that the star of the fifth trumpet is Satan. (Walvoord, Erdman, Fausset, J.B. Smith, Swete.)

There is another reason to believe that Satan is the instigator of the calamities seen in the blowing of the trumpets. In Revelation 12:4,7 the fraction one-third is closely associated with the extent of Satan's power. This fraction is found thirteen other times but always associated with the trumpets. Such a concentration of this fraction could not be coincidental. It must be symbolic—symbolic of Satan and his power.

Observe this remarkable association of Satan with the fraction one-third.

Revelation
8:7   third part of the trees were burnt up.
  8   third part of the sea became blood.
  9   third part of the creatures died.
  9   third part of the ships destroyed.
 10   third part of the rivers hit by fire.
 11   third part of the waters poisoned.
 12   third part of the sun darkened.
 12   third part of the moon darkened.
 12   third part of the stars darkened.
 12   third part of them was darkened.
 12   third part of the day, it did not shine.
9:15   slay the third part of men.
 18   third part of men were killed.
12:4   And his (Satan's) tail drew the third part of the stars (angels) of heaven.

Not only does one see this bizarre association of the fraction one-third with Satan and the blowing of the trumpets, but there is a third reason for incriminating Satan for the trumpet calamities. Note that the fourteen occurrences of the fraction one-third is always associated with destroying something good. In fact, in the blowing of the fifth trumpet, the name of the wicked agent is given in both Hebrew and Greek to emphasize that he is *Destroyer* (9:11). Throughout the Bible, beginning with the Garden of Eden, Satan is always seen as the wicked destroyer of the wonderful things that God has made.

Therefore, because of the three reasons just given, one can reasonably conclude that Satan is responsible for the calamities seen in the blowing of the first six trumpets. (See *Guide*, Appendix 22.) The time of these trumpets is the time of Satan's wrath (12:12 KJV).

9

THE ANTICHRIST FLIES INTO ACTION

Revelation 9:1–12

Three outstanding woes are announced in Revelation 8:13. Here is the first:

> Then the fifth angel blew his trumpet; and I saw a star that had fallen . . . to the earth, and the star was given the key of the shaft of the abyss. With this he opened the shaft of the abyss; and from the shaft smoke rose like smoke from a great furnace, and the sun and the air were darkened by the smoke from the shaft. . . . (9:1,2 NEB)

A star that had fallen to the earth. This star was first seen and described in Revelation 8:10. There, reasons were given to show that this star is a *symbol* of Satan. It cannot be a literal star as stars cannot receive keys nor open doors. It is also logical to believe that the key and the abyss mentioned here are symbolic terms.

What and where is this place called the abyss (Greek *abussos*)? Although this Greek word is explained in *Guide*, Appendix 23, a quick look is needed here. Abyss (bottomless pit) is used seven times in Revelation. But only twice elsewhere in the New Testament—a fact which indicates that it is not primarily a theological term! Literally, the word means a very deep place without a bottom —and nothing more. Figuratively, abyss seems to be the symbol in

Revelation of a country of bottomless iniquity.

Twice the word refers to the country from which the Antichrist emerges (11:7; 17:8). I say *country* because the Antichrist is a human being and must come from some nation on this earth. Three times abyss refers to the country from which flying agents emerge to torture people in another nation. To think of these flying agents arising out of some hollow place in the earth smacks too much of fantasy.

What country today would be the perfect fulfillment of this abyss—this place of unfathomable iniquity? That relevant question will be taken up later.

The Star (Satan) was given the key. Again note that nothing can happen until God's angels blow the trumpets and God releases the restraints that He has placed on this wicked country (2 Thessalonians 2:6–8 PHILLIPS). Also observe, as in all of the first six trumpets, that the destruction, torture, and death result from that sadistic activist—Satan. None of these trumpets are judgments of God but manifestations of the wrath of Satan (Revelation 12:12).

What happens when Satan hastens to release flying agents of torture on their cruel missions?

> . . .Then over the earth, out of the smoke, came locusts, and they were given the powers that earthly scorpions have. They were told to do no injury to the grass or to any plant or tree, but only to those men who had not received the seal of God on their foreheads. These they were allowed to torment for five months, with torment like a scorpion's sting; but they were not to kill them. During that time these men will seek death, but they will not find it; they will long to die, but death will elude them. (9:3–6 NEB)

Out of the smoke came locusts. It would appear that these flying agents emerge from a protective smoke screen. Such a maneuver is not new in twentieth-century warfare!

These flying agents were certainly *not* locusts because they did not eat any green vegetation. Their sole plan was to torment people. It seems probably that John called these high flying objects locusts because their shape and appearance were identical to locusts. In the detailed descriptions of these flying agents in the verses that follow, the apostle rules out their identity as locusts.

Only one class is protected from this torture of five months—the Israeli who were sealed (7:4) and heeded Jesus' admonition to flee (Matthew 24:16) and who escaped Satan's effort to catch them (12:6).

(See *Guide*, Appendix 19.) Because of the mention of Israeli here, one wonders if only Israel is hit by this trumpet. The same implication will be seen in the sixth trumpet.

John is seeing and describing an aerial invasion which is still in the future in our day and doing it with first-century words. That is not easy! He is painfully conscious of the limitations of his vocabulary. He keeps searching for a word that is not there. He likens everything to something of his day. Observe the frequent use of *like* (which I have italicized). If you were living before this century, I would not ask you this question, "What did John actually see?"

> In appearance the locusts were *like* horses equipped for battle. On their heads were what looked *like* golden crowns; their faces were *like* human faces and their hair *like* women's hair; they had teeth *like* lion's teeth, and wore breastplates *like* iron; the sound of their wings was *like* the noise of horses and chariots rushing to battle; they had tails *like* scorpions, with stings in them, and in their tails lay power to plague mankind for five months. (9:7–10 NEB)

Here John sees these flying machines at close range on the ground. *Like horses equipped for battle! Wore breastplates like iron.* John no doubt had seen Roman war steeds with protective metal armor. The metallic sheets were not exactly like the iron that John had seen. Could these have been lighter in color and thinner? My hat is off to John who was exceptionally expert in observing and describing what he saw with the only words that he had.

Their faces were like human faces. Vividly I recall the first jet plane that I saw. This huge monster slowly taxied into its boarding position. It was impressive, awesome! I was close to it. I must confess I was overawed! High on the front of it, I saw something that struck me as being weird—*a face like a human face.* In a second or two I recognized it as the face of the pilot. Perhaps, John never did!

They had teeth like lion's teeth. Years ago I was teaching this chapter to a college group. I confessed to them that I had no proper interpretation for "teeth like lion's teeth." "Spud" Belcher, a World War II pilot, promptly spoke up, "Ah yes, on the air intake of the jet engines there are metal slats that look much like a mouth with long teeth."

The sound of their wings was like the noise of horses and chariots rushing to battle. Congratulations, John, for a simile that everybody today can understand!

They had tails like scorpions. In Africa I saw scorpions with their upturned tails, an excellent replica to the upturned tail of a plane.

Tails . . . with stings in them. During World War II I was in Freetown, West Africa. There I was intrigued with a poster put out by the British Air Force. On it was a picture of the upturned tail of one of their fighter planes. In the tail were five machine guns. At the bottom of the poster was this caption from our verse: THERE WERE STINGS IN THEIR TAILS.

However, these aerial invaders that John saw will not kill people but will torment them with some sort of ray that will sting as fiercely as a scorpion's sting. Even stoical Africans, when stung, will yell and scream as loudly as they can.

What kind of a ray will planes of the future use to torture people? Nobody knows! It is worthwhile to note what science has today. One reads about the miraculous laser beam in the September 10, 1966, *Business Week.*

> Here is a beam of light that could be made hotter than
> the sun and focused to a dime-sized spot over a distance of a
> mile.

If a person were *stung* with a few of these beams, he might well wish he were dead. But this is only one of several horrific realities. Scientists are now studying how best to knock holes in the ozone layer above our atmosphere. Then the powerful ultraviolet rays from the sun could really sting people within the cone made by the hole. This is probably not the method used, as such beams, if strong enough, could kill vegetation, which destruction is not permitted here.

Observe the nature of the king who is directing the activities of these aerial invaders:

> They had for their king the angel of the abyss, whose name,
> in Hebrew is Abaddon, and in Greek, Apollyon, or the destroyer. (9:11 NEB).

Here John gives his name both in Hebrew and in Greek to emphasize his *destructive* nature. The Apostle Paul, speaking of the Antichrist, also calls him the "son of *destruction*" (Thessalonians 2:3). (See *Guide,* Appendix 24.)

Exactly who is this Destroyer, the King of the Abyss? One thinks first of Satan and his outstanding destructive nature already discussed in Revelation 8. But it is illogical to think of Satan from the outside unlocking the abyss if he is the king on the inside. That would make Satan play two roles at the same time.

It is more reasonable to think that the king (of this country designated the *abyss*) is the Antichrist. The Antichrist is the human replica of Satan, being possessed by Satan and having his power (13:4,5).

There is a second similarity between Paul's Antichrist and John's king of the Abyss. In Revelation 9:1,2 the king is restrained within his country until God permits Satan to release this king. Likewise, in speaking of the Antichrist, Paul states that he is kept from his destructive activities until divine restraints are removed:

> ... You will probably also remember how I used to talk about a "restraining power" which would operate until the time should come for the emergence of this man.
> Evil is already insidiously at work, but its activities are restricted until what I have called the "restraining power" is removed. When that happens the lawless man will be plainly seen. . . . (2 Thessalonians 2:5–8 PHILLIPS)

There is a third and the most important reason for believing that the king of the abyss is the Antichrist. Twice John specifically states that the *Antichrist* emerges from the country known as the abyss (11:7; 17:8). One can hardly conceive of this hard-fisted dictator coming from that country and not being the king of it.

To summarize, the king of the abyss is the Antichrist for three reasons:

1 Both are destroyers.
2 Both are restrained by God until He releases them.
3 Both come from the country called the Abyss.

In many Scriptures the Lord puts the spotlight on this wicked man —this Destroyer. He is wholly dedicated to destroy nations, people, society, family life, and all religions. This lawless man will destroy by the use of terrorism and violence. The Bible stresses his war against Israel and Christianity because he will be motivated and empowered by Satan.

What country today would be the ideal spawning ground for such an inhuman cruel person? If one looks over all the nations of the present, does one nation stand far above all others for this unenviable distinction of destroying nations, society, family life, morals, and Christianity? What nation would that be? (See *Guide*, Appendix 25.)

10

WHEN EAST CLASHES WITH WEST

Revelation 9:13–20

After describing the torture of people with the fifth trumpet, John writes about the next events:

> One terror now ends, but there are two more coming!
> The sixth angel blew his trumpet and I heard a voice speaking from the four horns of th
>
> e golden altar that stands before the throne of God,
> Saying to the sixth angel, "Release the four mighty demons held bound at the great River Euphrates." (9:12–14 LNT)

(See *Guide*, Appendix 26 for significance of the altar.)

The Euphrates River is mentioned from Genesis to Revelation; from the Garden of Eden to Armageddon (Revelation 16:12–16). To Abraham, God promised that his seed would have all the territory from the river of Egypt to the Euphrates River (Genesis 15:18). Over a thousand years later this remarkable prediction was realized (1 Kings 4:24).

Because of disobedience Israel lost control of all of this great expanse. For many long centuries the homeless Jews wandered over the earth, history's most pathetic spectacle! It wasn't until this century that the UN gave to the Jew a small part of his promised possession.

Previously we discussed the Six-Day War. Suffice to say that if Syria becomes involved in another war with Israel, as all current indications suggest, Israel may well expand herself to the Euphrates River.

Both in Revelation 9:14 and 16:12–16, the Euphrates River is the boundary on which is poised a vast army from the east on its way to Israel. From several considerations, it would appear that the Euphrates will be the boundary of Israel rather than a very big physical obstacle which it is not.

Release the four mighty demons. These four demonic forces can not advance a devastating army until God's angel blows the trumpet. Of these evil forces one reads further.

They had been kept in readiness for that year and month and day and hour, and now they were turned loose to kill a third of all mankind.

They led an army of 200,000,000 warriors—I heard an announcement of how many there were. (9:15–16 LNT)

That year and month and day and hour. God does not release these forces until He is split-second ready to do so.

They . . . kill a third of mankind. Instigated by Satan's demons, this great army is wholly responsible for the slaughter. God will punish them for this wanton destruction (11:8). As previously mentioned the events that follow the blowing of the trumpets are not judgments from God but are manifestations of the wrath of Satan.

Clearly four sadistic demons *incite* the leaders of this army to action (compare Revelation 16:14). No normal human being could have been so devilishly cruel as to kill and to torture many millions of people as did Lenin, Stalin, Hitler, and Khrushchev unless they had been controlled by sadistic demons or by Satan himself. Scriptures repeatedly show that the basic attitude of Satan and demons is destructive (Matthew 4:5,6; 15:22; 17:15–18; Luke 4:35; 8:27–33; John 13:27 with Matthew 27:5; Acts 19:15,16; 1 Peter 5:8; *Guide*, Appendix 21 and 22).

One-quarter of the earth's population perished with the opening of the seals—850 million (6:8). With the blowing of this trumpet a third of the remaining three-fourths would mean the killing of another 850 million men, women, and children. Because such astronomical figures are most unlikely with conventional weapons of the past, one must conclude that in this future war there will be nuclear, chemical, biological, or geophysical weapons. One can understand why older generations considered such figures much too fantastic to be literal. But now these huge figures are much like those suggested by military experts without a shrug of the shoulders!

An army of 200,000,000! Even a few decades ago commentators called an army of 200 million fanciful, grotesque, impossible! The same idea was in John's mind when he reassured the reader, "I heard the number."

Even today the population of the Orient, exclusive of Russia, is 1.3 billion. This is 6½ times the size of the army mentioned. Furthermore, not only is the world's greatest population in the Far East, but there is a very high birth rate.

Also remember that the plagues that formerly ravaged the Orient have now largely been brought under control. In one city of India with

225,000 people, the World Health Organization gave BCG tuberculin vaccination to 210,814 people, nearly the entire population. The medical profession of the United States cannot boast of such a remarkable feat in preventing disease.

Lest any scoff at the Far East (Japan, China, India, and the others) being able to muster an army of 200 million in the future, may I suggest he read *Time* which reported that *one* of these nations, China, claimed that she alone could muster a man-woman militia of 200 million—and this was in 1965!

Yes, John, all the factual evidence points to the conclusion that you did hear the number correctly.

Where is this huge army going and with whom is it going to tangle? Scriptures indicate that just before the Euphrates episode, Russia (Gog) will invade Israel (Ezekiel 38 and 39); massacre two-thirds of the people (Zechariah 13:8); and then capture Jerusalem (Zechariah 14:2). Then ". . . tidings out of the east . . . shall trouble him," the Antichrist (Daniel 11:44). Could these *tidings out of the east* be this vast army from the Orient crossing the Euphrates River?

Daniel states that when the Antichrist with his utterly godless forces goes north from Jerusalem, he sets up his headquarters at Armageddon (Daniel 11:45). Since Ezekiel states twice that these forces come from their "place out of the north parts," these invaders must be Russian (Ezekiel 38:15; 39:2 ASV). Currently Russia and China are very hostile to each other. Armageddon appears to be the center of the arena where these two godless nations will assault each other with everything that they possess. Although the broad well-watered plain at Armageddon is the meeting place, the battlefield will cover a distance of at least two hundred miles (Revelation 14:20).

When John describes the military hardware of this great army, he has only first-century words to describe what he sees. No doubt he had seen Roman war steeds covered with armor, and these war horses came the closest to describing the moving, warring agents that he now sees. Hence, he calls them horses. But his description indicates that he is painfully aware of their being entirely different. Decide yourself what John actually did see:

> I saw their horses spread out before me in my vision; their riders wore fiery-red breastplates, though some were sky-blue and others yellow. The horses' heads looked much like lions', and smoke and fire and flaming sulphur bellowed from their mouths, killing one-third of all mankind.
>
> Their power of death was not only in their mouths, but in

71

their tails as well, for their tails were similar to serpents' heads that struck and bit with fatal wounds. (9:17–19 LNT)

What kind of a killing agent is this? Throwing out flames and poison gas from the front! And from the tail a striking and biting power that kills people!

Was John looking at a modern tank equipped with flame throwers and poison gas? From the rear of these armored vehicles were long extensions "similar to serpents' heads that struck with fatal wounds." How accurately that describes a tank's long rear guns with their bulbous muzzles!

I think the Apostle John deserves a very special award for meticulous reporting, and I believe you will also agree that the prophet Joel should have the same award. If you study the chart on the day of God's wrath, you will observe that both John and Joel are describing the *same* battle. Read the following description to see if the prophet Joel also saw twentieth-century tanks in action.

> . . . here comes a huge host in power,
> blackening the hills;
> the like of it never has been,
> the like of it never shall be . . .
> before them fire devouring,
> behind them flames a-blazing;
> before them the land lies like an Eden paradise,
> behind them it is a desolate desert—
> for nothing escapes them.
> They look like horses,
> they run like war-horses,
> as chariots rattle,
> they leap on the hill-tops,
> like flames that crackle, consuming the straw,
> like a vast army in battle array.
> Hearts are in anguish before them,
> all faces turn pale.
> They charge like warriors,
> they advance like fighters,
> each on his own track—
> no tangling of paths—
> none pushes his fellow,
> each follows his own line;
> they burst through weapons unbroken,

they rush on the city, run over the walls. . . . (Joel 2:2–9
MOFFATT)

John called them horses; Joel said, "They look like horses." But both described these as being very different. Both John and Joel were impressed by the deadly devastation and by the flames that burned everything to a barren crisp. Only nuclear bombs can exceed the incendiary power of napalm. Napalm transforms people into nearly inextinguishable torches. It is such a highly efficient killer that it will undoubtedly be used into the 1980s and perhaps beyond, as expert Nigel Calder points out in *Unless Peace Comes.*

The allies used incendiary bombs in World War II—at Dresden, Germany, where three hundred thousand were burned to death in one night; at Hamburg where seventy thousand died; and in Tokyo with the death of two hundred thousand, reports Piel in *The Fallen Sky.*

Flaming sulphur bellowed from their mouths. Poison gases were first used on a large scale in World War I. In 1914 the French used tear gas but the Germans were the first to use poison gas (chlorine) in 1915. Then followed the more deadly ones such as mustard gas.

It was during World War II that exceedingly deadly gases were discovered. The most lethal were the nerve gases. Consider one of these—sarin. Adults can be killed by as little as 0.7 mg. within a few minutes. It is odorless. Gas masks are useless as it is readily absorbed through the skin. It is so very deadly that one expert, Nigel Calder, states, "It will probably rank high among the gas weapons of the 1980s." Although scientists of many nations have been working feverishly to develop newer gases, they feel that in this nerve gas they have just about the ultimate in killing power.

In the case of this vast army from the Far East, the use of flame throwers and poison gas play an important role. This army is headed for Armageddon in Israel (Revelation 16:16).

Killing one-third of all mankind. As previously stated that would mean about 850 million. That would include the civilian deaths on both sides, a conservative figure when one remembers that one-half of the people of the world live in the Orient. John next describes the attitude of the survivors:

But the men left alive after these plagues *still refused to worship God!*
They would not renounce their demon-worship, nor their

idols made of gold and silver, brass, stone and wood—which neither see nor hear nor walk! (9:20 LNT)

Refusing to worship God, people in the last days will turn to the dark unseen realm controlled by Satan. Of course, men have dabbled for ages in the frightening world of demonic spirits. But in civilized society their numbers have been comparatively insignificant. But this verse indicates that worship of Satanic demons and their idolatrous symbols will characterize the last days. Instead of demon worship being the exception to the norm, it seems that it will be the accepted pattern of the last days.

How close is society today to the pattern predicted by the Lord? In the past few years many groups given to such worship have mushroomed! Only a few of the largest can be mentioned here.

First, Satanism! Worshippers of Satan are meeting regularly in their so-called churches all over the country. Traditionally the members gather around an altar where a naked "virgin" lies on a fur rug. As bells ring and an organ booms, Satan dressed in scarlet satin makes a dramatic entrance. While he chants from a satanic bible, the congregation joins with appropriate responses. Members are asked to express their innermost lusts. Then with an air of authority, Satan proclaims, "May all your lustful thoughts reach fruition!"

In October, 1969, Walter Cronkite televised parts of such a service. Viewers must have cringed as the members of the church loudly chanted, "Hail Satan, hail Satan, hail Satan!" This particular group in California claims seven thousand members. One of the leaders interviewed was the president of a Parent Teachers Association.

And from the January 5, 1968, issue of *Time* is this observation:

Black Magic is very "In" among some hippies, as is devil worship. There are even witches and warlocks around Hashbury ready to celebrate Black masses in praise of Satan. Traditional ritual requires the presence of a naked virgin—and there aren't many in communal crash pads.

Actually there are hundreds of cults of the occult seeking guidance, not from God's Holy Spirit, but from the spirit realm of Satan, from such agents as demons, witches, and mediums which are repeatedly denounced by God (Exodus 22:18; Deuteronomy 18:10; 1 Samuel 28:-7–9; Micah 5:12; Nahum 3:4).

Today, mysticism is popular and many practices of ancient rites are being experimented with in various forms. The worshipers often sit cross-legged in incense-clouded rooms with candles.

The *New York Times*, describing Sybil Leek as "perhaps the world's best known witch," quotes her as saying that there are more than four hundred witch covens (circles of thirteen witches) operating in the United States.

Also the National Council of Churches knows of well over four hundred spiritualist churches with at least 150,000 members. There are many more spiritualist groups which meet secretly. And there is a far greater number of disturbed people who resort to these spiritualist mediums from time to time to obtain answers to their many problems.

Published by the American Medical Association, *Today's Health* (November, 1970) reports:

An estimated 40 million Americans aided by 5000 astrologers have helped turn the zodiac into a $200-million-a-year business . . . Some 1200 of the country's 1750 daily newspapers now carry astrology columns. . . . Sales of occult books have doubled in the past three years. A book about Jeane Dixon . . . has sold more than three million copies. Bookstores and specialty stores sell everything from magical charms and mystical games to volumes on *Sorcery Self-Taught*. Last year (1969) these stores sold over two million Ouija boards. A Ouija board, of course, is used in seeking spiritualistic or telepathic messages.

How close is civilized man to the Lord's prediction of the last days: "The men . . . refused to worship God. They would not renounce their demon-worship, nor their idols . . . which neither see nor hear nor walk"?

Certainly, nobody should look askance at the Lord's predictions of such worship in the last days (9:20; 13:4,12–15; 14:9; 19:20). Instead, they should sense the imminence of "the last days." Yes, and thank the Lord for enabling them to *discern these times*.

Outstanding psychiatrists have studied and agree on the reason for this tremendous increase of delving into the spirit world. (See *Guide*, Appendix 27 for their findings.)

In the next chapter one discovers that some of the most perplexing problems of this century were also predicted: drug-abuse, immorality, and crime.

11

DRUGS, IMMORALITY, CRIME—ALL PREDICTED

As eight of us physicians studied a University of Buffalo sophomore, we listened to his story. Four days before, he and his roommate had eaten the seeds from a certain flower. "Just for kicks!"

The next morning he started off to his class. He had to cross busy Main Street. To him the cars seemed to be traveling "a thousand miles an hour and the people seemed to be walking about a hundred miles an hour." Guardian angels must have been busy getting him across that street.

That morning his professor gave a test. He looked at the paper but it made no sense. He then decided to go to the university's health center.

Here is the rest of his story. "When I entered the examining room, the nurses grabbed me and put me into a big pot of oil and fixed me so that I couldn't get out. Then one of them lit a fire under that pot and started to boil me.

"I never suffered such agony in my whole life. It was worse than hell fire. Then the nurse came at me with a long butcher knife. She took it and cut off all the flesh from my arms and legs—right down to my bones. The pain was awful. I must have fainted then. I didn't know anything until I woke up in this awful place."

"This awful place" was an institution for the insane!

There are over half a dozen drugs that can cause such hallucinations. The insanity usually clears up in time. LSD is the most dangerous of the hallucinogenic drugs. In fact, it is ten times stronger than the active ingredient in the seeds just mentioned.

Yet in the 1964–1967 period certain intellectuals promoted LSD as a safe drug. Dr. Timothy Leary, a Harvard psychologist, used it extensively in his sex-oriented groups near Boston and then later in Mexico until both Harvard and Mexico put him out.

LSD lessens one's natural inhibitions. A professor of a Philadelphia university came out of his LSD spree to discover that he had been running naked and bleeding up and down his boulevard.

Four teen-agers on a binge with LSD rammed into a house and killed a three-year-old. In jail, the driver was in such a psychedelic trance that he tried to climb up the wall as he yelled, "I'm a graham cracker; see, my arm just crumbled off."

The insanity produced by LSD can fill the individual with such imaginary fears that he may kill others or himself.

One person exclaimed, "I am the universe! I am all men!" Such feelings of omnipotence or an exaggerated sense of power is common. A number have felt so capable that they have walked out of high windows without any fear or walked in front of speeding cars with confidence.

Grief-stricken Art Linkletter, speaking of his lovely daughter who jumped from a sixth-floor apartment window, said, "It wasn't a suicide because Dianne wasn't herself. It was murder. She was murdered by the people who manufacture and sell LSD."

Yes, and one might add that the accomplices to such tragedies are those who create devastating violence in demanding that legal restrictions be removed from psychedelic drugs. Government agencies have repeatedly shown that the instigators of half a dozen lawless campus groups are Marxist—dedicated to destroying society. One must give Red Communism credit for insight in selecting such a powerful weapon as psychedelic drugs to demoralize a nation from within and render it vulnerable for an easy capture.

In the category of narcotic drugs, heroin is king. It is different from the drugs just considered. Heroin produces a powerful physical dependence. If the addict cannot obtain his drug, he suffers intolerable cramps and other distressing complaints. Also, heroin must be taken in ever increasing doses to get the desired effect.

For this reason the cost of the daily dose keeps spiraling. It varies from $15 to $200 a day with an average in one study of $75 a day. Other studies averaged about $40. To obtain that kind of money the addict will hazard daring bank robberies or commit other heinous crimes to satisfy his overpowering craving and relieve his severe pains. According to *The Attack*, depending on the geographical area, 15 percent to 50 percent of major crimes are committed by heroin addicts. They steal $1 billion worth of goods each year, according to the National Association of Blue Cross Plans. Their families soon go on welfare as most of the addicts eventually become unproductive. The suppliers of these drugs become powerfully rich and often corrupt police and politicians.

The girls who get hooked sometimes turn to crime, most frequently to prostitution. In fact, an extremely high percentage of prostitutes are probably drug addicts.

In New York City alone, overdosages of heroin account for one to three deaths a day. Recently a twelve-year-old boy was such a victim.

Attention should be called to the close association of drugs, immorality, and crime because these same three vices are given as signs of the last days. The relevant Scripture will be given shortly but keep these three interlocked sins in mind while reading about the next drug.

The drug most commonly abused today is marihuana, usually called pot. The strongest form is hashish. A teen-ager pressures his mother, "Mom, everybody smokes pot!" Donald B. Louria states in *Drug Abuse: A Current Assessment*: "Some high schools and colleges now report a prevalence in the 70 to 80 percent range. It appears that the majority of these students only experiment with marihuana but a substantial minority use the drug habitually." Some colleges and universities have about 10 percent psychologically addicted but Christian colleges have only a very insignificant number smoking it.

A survey in *Medical World News* of two medical schools indicated that in one school only 5 percent "turn on with pot," but 17 percent in that school stated that they would use it if the law did not have such stiff penalties. In the other medical school, 44 percent currently use pot and 57 percent would if it were not for the law.

Marihuana can best be described as an unpredictable drug acting on unpredictable people with unpredictable results. It is an unpredictable drug because the percentage of the active agent, THC, varies greatly with the hemp plant itself and with the nature of the soil and the temperature. One product can be sixty times as strong as another. Furthermore, sellers of the drug not infrequently spike it with addictive drugs. For these reasons there is a great deal of controversy over the harmfulness and the effects of the drug. Nothing is standardized about marihuana.

Furthermore, the *people* who use pot are very unpredictable. One teen-ager reports, "Two of us were walking down the street and we both were high on pot. All of a sudden he leaped into the air and then ran into a filling station. For no reason at all he began to beat up the attendant. He was like a wild man. We had to call the police."

Furthermore, in a case of borderline insanity, marihuana may be enough to push an individual from the realm of reality to a psychotic state.

Unpredictable reactions sometimes occur with marihuana. Three types of exceptions to pleasurable effects are: simple depressive reactions, panic reactions, and toxic psychosis, according to Andrew T. Weil, M.D. The panic reactions are the most common. The user thinks he is removed from reality. It is very frightening as he is sure he is losing his mind or is leaving this earth by dying. Toxic psychosis (insanity) is fortunately not as common but Boston University's Dr. R.E.

Pillard writes, "Toxic psychosis precipitated by marihuana, has frequently been reported." One cannot tell whether pot will give a "trip" or a tragedy.

The majority of people who smoke pot have euphoria (feelings of elation and a false sense of security and ability). Because of this effect people tend to smoke pot whenever unpleasant situations arise in their unlovely world of reality. They escape these by taking a trip into the more pleasant world of fantasy. But it is an escape to nowhere! It is a chemically induced daydream. Because of this pleasant escape any person may develop a psychological dependence for the drug. Hence, pot can well be called the crutch that cripples.

Users of pot tend to giggle and laugh over childish trifles, especially in a group setting. There is also an altered sense of time and space, qualities absolutely essential in driving a car and operating machinery. This fact explains the increase of motor vehicle and other accidents in pot users. Large doses of pot can also produce hallucinations. Pot can transform an energetic person into a big blob of inertia, not interested in work, study, or play.

Smoking pot does not create a craving for heroin. But close association with those who sell pot is bad as these pushers either sell or have connections with those who deal in heroin.

One pot user reports, "You smoke a stick of marihuana in the morning, get lazy on the job, and get fired. In my case it led to fixing with heroin."

Another reports, "The first time I took heroin was when I found I was out of marihuana."

Dr. B.E. Leonard cites in a British journal a survey of 124 opiate addicts of whom 80 percent had started off with marihuana. In Chapple's series of 80 opiate addicts, all had used pot first (reported in the same journal).

Authorities disagree on many aspects of the effects of marihuana, yet one reads: "The various scientific and medical committees that have studied the matter have come to a surprisingly unanimous conclusion: that marihuana should not be legalized for general consumption, but that harsh penalties are unwise." (Richard C. Pillard)

I was shocked as I listened to a professor of a theological seminary in the Chicago area speak to a dedicated group of Christian workers. He extolled Margaret Mead and her ideas about the harmlessness of marihuana. Why does a certain type of theologian always gravitate to anti-Scriptural viewpoints while ignoring the objective findings of outstanding authorities?

Furthermore, the immorality involved in the use of pot is the most devastating effect of all because it is the most widespread. It results from *marihuana's well recognized ability to lessen man's natural inhibitions.* Even a dictionary brings out that fact in defining *psychedelic* —"causing an exposure of normally repressed psychic elements." Marihuana, the most widely used of the psychedelic drugs can also increase one's susceptibility to suggestions.

Visualize behind locked doors a mixed group all high on pot. Consider a newcomer to the pot party. With the brakes off his natural inhibitions and his mind chemically open to suggestions, he is somewhat like a person in a hypnotic trance—a victim of what he hears and sees. Suggestions are there in the swingy music with its sex and drug oriented words. Under the influence of pot both words and music take on a seemingly ethereal beauty.

Suggestions that would have been repulsive before smoking the pot now take on a halo of plausibility and decency. He sees others undress and go into action. With a dreamy uninhibited mind open to suggestions and with a yearning near-naked partner at his side, the result is fairly predictable.

Surely the close association of drugs and immorality should be evident. John the Apostle predicted this widespread association of drugs and immorality.

Christians must kick themselves awake so that they can discern and do something about the drugs ready to devastate the bodies, brains, and the souls of the truly wonderful and talented young people of Christian society—the only hope for civilization. Christians must realize that drugs, immorality, and crime make up a mighty, syndicated steamroller that is flattening out all morals and destroying the family and civilized society. In the wake of these immoral ravagers is an epidemic of venereal diseases much too vast for the medical profession to control properly.

When Christians can discern in all of this moral crackup the fulfillment of the signs of the last days, their faith in God and His Word will not fail but only be strengthened. Because the church has not been discerning, it has passed through these successive attitudes regarding immorality: utter repulsion, silent endurance, then feeble excusing, and now recently acceptance. Two excellent articles in *Christianity Today* (September 11, 1970) reveal how professed Christians are now accepting sexual promiscuity and homosexuality.

Because of the crumbling moral standards in the last third of this century, I feel compelled to speak out with a medical frankness that may shock some good people. I offer no apologies since few voices are heard to counteract the subtle propaganda designed to entice everybody into drug traps.

Perhaps the most attractive bait used to catch the naïve was the promise of very exciting and colorful sexual experiences. Dr. Timothy Leary was quoted as saying that LSD was the most powerful sexual stimulant known to man. With such attractive bait and the assurance that LSD was perfectly safe, countless thousands ran headlong after the Pied Pipers of dope, many to their doom.

The irony of it all is that neither LSD, marihuana, nor any psychedelic drug increases anybody's sexual prowess. If a person was impotent before, he will be just as impotent afterward. The more these drugs are dissolved in the blood, the weaker the sex urge.

A couple using marihuana was questioned as they came out of a pad. The male was lethargic and sleepy, yet bragging of his colorful experience; but his partner described the whole affair as a frustrating attempt that meant nothing to either one.

Philip K. Kaufman describes the futile, frustrating sexuality of the pad in the *New York State Journal of Medicine:*

> With sex exploration there is movement onto the pads.
> Pad groups encourage many shifting arrangements, rarely
> any close relationships. They seek to use sex and drugs
> as prime tools of involvement. All kinds of drugs and
> partners are experimented with in this compulsive
> search for emotional closeness. As normal sex deteriorates,
> the more bizarre forms take over.

Normal sex deteriorates. Sex mixed with lust always deteriorates. Sex mixed with divine love glows and endures. One would expect just that since it was God who built the sex urge into man. And God also gave man a Guide Book so that he might obtain from sex the superlatives: the most, the best, and for the longest time. What class of people enjoy sex into the eighth and ninth decade of life? Usually it is a couple who follow the directives in the best sex manual ever written—the Bible!

It is true that a number of psychedelic drugs remove the natural built-in inhibitions about sex. Under their influence cultured people will lie down with unkempt, unwashed, odorous specimens of humanity alive with crawling pubic lice and suffering with venereal disease.

A very cultured young woman said to her husband, "Let's become animals." What a mess they made for themselves! A mess that will torture them to their graves. This mature couple and the immature adolescents on the hippie pads never even suspect that in their obnoxious perversions they are either marring or, more often, destroying one of God's choice gifts to men and women.

Even the world is dizzy and aghast at the unprecedented and widespread increase of psychedelic drugs, immorality, and crime. Of course, all three have existed from the fall of man, but the interlocking and the world-wide spiraling of all three are most significant since these three vices have been signaled and predicted for the last days of this age.

Psychedelic drugs predicted in the Bible? Those who assume that God's prophets did not know anything about such drugs should be reminded that opium was used before history was written. The psychological effects of opium may have been known to the ancient Sumerians (4,000 B.C.) whose ideograph for the poppy was "joy plant." Historians suspect that it may have been called the joy plant because of the euphoria produced by the opium extract.

Be that as it may, indisputable reference to opium is found in the writings of Theophrastus in the third century B.C. according to Goodman and Gilman in *The Pharmacological Basis of Therapeutics*. Records of psychedelic drugs appear throughout history. The Crusaders carried marihuana while the Turkish sultans smoked the strong resinous extract known as hashish in their pipes.

Webster gives an intriguing glimpse of hashish in his definition of the word *assassin*.

> assassin . . . [Arabic *hashshashin* plural of *hashshash* one addicted to hashish.] Capitalized: a secret order of Muslims that at the time of the Crusades terrorized Christians and other enemies by secret murder committed under the influence of hashish.

Lucy Kavaler has written an intriguing book, *Mushrooms, Molds, and Miracles*. One chapter deals with psychedelic drugs obtained from such fungi. This chapter describes how Iceland and Scandinavian countries were terrorized by drug-crazed murderers between the ninth and twelfth centuries. These gangs were called the Berserks after a hero who wore only a bearskin to battle. According to the history of this period these gangs of Berserks would suddenly act like wild frenzied animals with superhuman strength. They would suddenly have fits of shivering and chills in which their faces would swell and change color. Then they would howl, bite their shields, and start killing mercilessly. As these murderous seizures slackened they would be stupid and very weak for several days.

These seizures resembled the actions of a murderous psychopath except they all recovered after a short period. Furthermore, in A.D. 1123 a law was passed exiling for three years anyone who went berserk. From then on these murderous attacks were no longer reported.

Historians now suspect that on the day of a massacre, the men would eat the mushroom *Amanita muscaria,* which contains a powerful psychedelic drug. Kavaler states that this mushroom flourishes in many parts of the world and cites many other historical incidents about its use.

Hippocrates (460?–377? B.C.) prescribed the juice of the poppy capsules for their physical and psychological effects. Early Greek physicians also wrote about the strong addictive powers that opium possessed.

The Apostle John brings out four times in Revelation that drugs will be used for evil purposes in the last days of this age (Revelation 9:21; 18:23; 21:8; 22:15). The Greek words are *pharmakeia* (used twice), *pharmakeus,* and *pharmakos.* I asked Dr. F. Gordon Stockin to give me the meaning of *pharmakeia* as used in classical Greek. He stated that the primary meaning of the word is "the use of drugs," while the secondary meaning is "using drugs for a foul purpose."

Commenting on the use of *pharmakeia* in Revelation 9:21, New Testament scholars also bear down on the fact that this word is definitely drug-oriented. See the *Commentary* of Jamieson, Fausset and Brown; Dr. A.T. Robertson's *Word Pictures in the New Testament;* and both Young's and Strong's *Analytical Concordances.*

Robertson writes that originally *pharmakeia* meant "enchantment," but later, "drug." Young in his lexicon combines these two concepts and defines *pharmakeia* as "enchantment with drugs."

I have presented the foregoing to say this: the common translations of such a word as *pharmakeia* pathetically ignores the fact that *pharmakeia* is a drug-oriented word. In the four occurrences of this word and its related forms in Revelation, it is translated *sorceries* or *sorcers.*

There is another Greek word *mageia* with its related forms that is properly translated sorceries or sorcerer. *Mageia,* from which the word *magic* comes, is found nowhere in Revelation.

One should not think that John and others in the first century were unfamiliar with "enchanting" or psychedelic drugs. Roman soldiers carried marihuana with them.

With these explanations, now insert Young's translation of *pharmakeia* into a paraphrased reading of Revelation 9:21:

> And they did not repent of their murders, or their *enchantment with drugs* or their sexual vice or their thefts.

The context of this verse shows that the time is that of the sixth trumpet, just preceeding the return of the Lord to this earth in great wrath. The people living then will not be using psychedelic drugs for helpful curative purposes, but will be using them as vicious accessories to their sexual vice, murders, and thefts. Commenting on the fact that our word *pharmacy* comes from the same Greek root as *pharmakeia*, A. T. Robertson writes, "Our word *pharmacy* as applied to drugs and medicine has certainly come a long way out of a bad environment." A bad environment indeed, intimately intertwined with sexual vice and crime! In the first part of this chapter I attempted to show how psychedelic drugs, sexual vice, and crime synergistically work for a common goal—the destruction of mankind.

Of course, man has had these vices from the fall of Adam but only recently has the world witnessed such a widespread flood of psychedelic drugs, such epidemic flagrant immorality, such an unprecedented increase of crime! And all interlocked for a common fiendish purpose.

It was not the purpose of this writer to imply that man is now living in the time of the blowing of the sixth trumpet, but no one can deny that the world stage is being rapidly set for the enactment of the events of that day.

Finally, this writer cannot claim any originality for his interpretation of Revelation 9:21. Over a hundred years ago J.A. Seiss wrote a three-volume commentary on Revelation, a classic widely read. Seiss does not show that *pharmakeia* is a drug-oriented word, yet he assumes it, and devotes three pages to amplify that interpretation. Elaborating on what the Apostle John predicted in Revelation 9:21, he truly painted an accurate picture of our day:

> Murder will be among the commonest of crimes. Sensual and selfish passion will make sad havoc of human life. . . . Feticide [abortion], infanticide, homicide, and all forms of sin against human life will characterize society, and be tolerated and passed as if no great harm were done. . . . Sorceries, impure practices with evil agencies, and particularly with poisonous drugs, is given as one of the dominant forms of vice and sin in those days. The word [*pharmakeia*] specially includes tampering with one's own and another's health, by means of drugs, potions, intoxications, and often with magical arts and incantations . . . the putting under influences promotive of sins of impurity both bodily and spiritual. We have only to think of the use of . . . medicaments to increase love attractions, of resorts to the pharmacopeia in connection with sensuality . . . of the growing prevalence of crime induced by these things, setting loose and stimulating to activity the vilest passions,

which are eating out the moral sense of society,—for the beginnings of that moral degeneracy to which the seer here alludes as characteristic of the period when the sixth trumpet is sounded.

And interlinked with these . . . will also be the general subversion of marriage and its laws, and deluging of society with the sins of fornication and adultery. The Apostle uses the word "fornication" alone, as embracing all forms of lewdness, but as if to intimate that marriage will then be hardly recognized any more.

12

MAN'S MOST THRILLING DAY

Revelation 10

I asked a college group to select the most thrilling day of their entire existence. Would it be the day of their conversion, the day of their marriage, or the day of their resurrection from the dead? Overwhelmingly they voted for the day of their resurrection. That day is called the Rapture because of its glory, jubilance, and ecstasy.

Yet if one would ask the average Christian to tell all he knows about the Rapture and the events that precede and follow it, his knowledge would scarcely fill a thimble. He knows little or nothing about the most glorious day of his existence!

This chapter seeks to correct that deficiency. After reading the frightening display of Satan's wrath in the two previous chapters, one will be refreshed to bask in the glory of this chapter.

Then I saw another mighty angel descending from Heaven. He was clothed in a cloud, and there was a rainbow around his head. His face blazed like the sun, his legs like pillars of fire, and he had a little book lying open in his hand. He planted his right foot on the sea and his left foot on the land, and then shouted with a loud voice like the roar of a lion. And when he shouted the seven thunders lifted their voices. When the seven thunders had rolled I was on the point of writing but I heard a voice from Heaven, saying,

"Seal up what the seven thunders said, but do not write it down!" (10:1–4 PHILLIPS)

Recently I sailed past the harbor of Rhodes, about a hundred miles south of John's Patmos. I tried to visualize what the great Colossus of Rhodes must have resembled. This monstrous bronze statue of Helios the Sun God, was over 100 feet high, as high as a ten-story building. When one realizes that it was constructed in 280 B.C., it is understandable why it was one of the seven wonders of the ancient world. It fell in an earthquake in 224 B.C.

But the personage that the Apostle John saw was living. He was much higher and more awe-inspiring, so high that he was clothed with a cloud and had a rainbow around his head. His face blazed like the sun. His legs were pillars of fire with one foot on the land while the other stood upon the sea.

Who is this mighty being? Remember that the Greek word *aggelos* can be translated *angel, messenger,* or *agent.* The context determines the proper choice.

Does the description of this outstanding personage seem to fit one of the billions of angels? Nowhere in the Bible is any angel described so minutely and with designations reserved elsewhere for Deity. If one compares these distinctions with the prophetic descriptions of our Lord, he will be surprised and impressed with the similarities. (See *Guide,* Appendix 28.)

Three times one is told that this personage has one foot on the sea and the other on the land. Such a posture and such repetition symbolize and emphasize His ownership and authority over all the earth and the seven seas. His right hand raised in the heavens indicates His control there.

His voice, similar to the awesome roar of a lion, seems to challenge every earthly ruler. The resounding affirmation of the seven thunders reminds one of the seven voices of Jehovah in Psalm 29. There His voice "thundereth . . . upon many waters . . . breaketh the cedars . . . shaketh the wilderness" (KJV).

Then the angel whom I had seen bestriding the sea and the land raised his right hand to Heaven and swore by the living one of the timeless ages, who created Heaven, earth and sea and all that is in them. (10:5,6 PHILLIPS)

To dispel any doubts as to the certainty of the promise now to be given, this mighty Messenger raises His right hand to heaven and solemnly swears. Lest one think that the making of such an oath disproves the identity of Christ, he should read this:

> For when God gave the promise to Abraham, since He had no greater to swear by, He swore by Himself . . . to display more convincingly to the heirs of the promise how unchangeable His purpose was. . . . (Hebrews 6:13,17 WEYMOUTH)

In Genesis 22:15,16 where the identity of Deity is evident, the Lord is referred to as an *angel*. Both there and here in Revelation 10:6 this so-called angel takes an oath to clinch His unchangeable promises. Why? The promise about to be given here is beamed primarily to Christians living during the tribulation and facing death and life issues. Some are facing martyrdom for themselves and their families. Such people need the absolute assurance that only an infallible Christ under oath can give. Many angels have failed (Revelation 12:4,7) but the promise and oath of the Lord Himself give the ultimate in assurance.

After such emphasis on His appearance, His posture, and His oath, His promise must have commanding significance:

> . . . there shall be delay no longer: but in the days of the voice of the seventh angel, when he is about to sound, then is finished the mystery of God, according to the good tidings which he declared to his servants the prophets. (10:6,7 ASV)

Indeed, this is a short but most important message. Like the carefully chosen words of an international cablegram!

When he is about to sound. Berkeley translators put it, "when he is at the point of blowing." Observe the split second timing of this happening.

Just seconds *before* the last trump is sounded, a great event, called a mystery, is going to be realized. This mystery is the long-awaited fulfillment of "the good tidings" declared by the prophets.

Observe, please, that the Apostle Paul calls this event by the same name, "a mystery," and also states that it occurs at the time of the "last trump."

> Behold, I shew you a mystery; We shall not all sleep [die], but we shall all be changed,
> In a moment, in the twinkling of an eye, at the last trump . . . . (1 Corinthians 15:51,52 KJV)

The descriptions of the Apostles Paul and John are strikingly similar.

1 Both call it a mystery.
2 Both give the time as that of the last trumpet.
3 Both relate the time to the end of this age.
4 Both indicate that it is a time of rejoicing.

To me it is thrilling that Job, suffering in the direst of tribulation, encouraged himself in the same "blessed hope."

> For I know that my redeemer liveth, and that he shall stand at the latter day upon the earth:
> And though after my skin worms destroy this body, yet in my flesh shall I see God. (Job. 19:25,26 KJV)

The Apostle Paul predicts as a prophet.

> For the Lord himself shall descend from heaven, with a shout . . . and with the trump of God: and the dead in Christ shall rise first; then we that are alive, that are left, shall together with them be caught up in the clouds, to meet the Lord in the air: and so shall we ever be with the Lord. Wherefore comfort one another with these words. (1 Thessalonians 4:16–18 ASV)

The Great Prophet Jesus foretold the same blessed day:

> Then shall two men be in the field; one is taken, and one is left: two women shall be grinding at the mill; one is taken and one is left. Watch therefore: for ye know not on what day your Lord cometh. (Matthew 24:40–42 ASV)

This Rapture has ever been a mystery to those in darkness but a bright and blessed hope to the Christian. It occurs just at the moment when the "last trump" is "about to sound." Now observe what happens when the last trumpet actually sounds:

> . . .The seventh angel blew his trumpet . . . now thy wrath has come and with it the time for the dead to be judged and for reward to be given to thy servants, the prophets and the saints, and all who fear thy name, both small and great. Now is the time for destroying the destroyers of the earth! (11:15,18 PHILLIPS)

It is important to observe that the Rapture occurs before the wrath of God is poured out on the world—the Rapture is definitely pre-wrath. This timing is also seen in Revelation 19 where the union of Christ with His Bride occurs, again just *before* the wrath of God is poured on a wicked world. It is significant that both chapters present the Rapture as occurring just before the wrath of God. Other Scriptures support this view (Matthew 24:29–31; John 5:24–29; 1 Thessalonians 4:16–5:3).

In the chart below, Revelation 10:7 and 11:18 are compared with other Scriptures generally accepted as referring to the Rapture. There is no better way to evaluate a passage than to compare Scripture with Scripture. Careful study of these passages provides rich dividends.

COMPARATIVE RELEVANCY OF RAPTURE SCRIPTURES

Characteristics of the Rapture	I Cor. 15 23-52	I Thess. 4:16-5:11	2 Thess. 2: 1-12	Matt. 24: 27-51	John 5: 24-29	Rev. 10:7; 11:18	Rev. 4:1
Time of blowing of the trumpet	Yes	Yes		Yes		Yes	
Return of Christ to earth	Yes	Yes	Yes	Yes	Yes	Yes	
Resurrection stated or implied	Yes	Yes	Yes		Yes	Yes	
Rejoicing for the righteous	Yes	Yes	Yes	Yes	Yes	Yes	
Event called a mystery	Yes					Yes	
Punishment for the living wicked		Yes	Yes	Yes	Yes	Yes	
Numerical value of Rapture Scriptures	5 Characteristics	5 Characteristics	4 Characteristics	4 Characteristics	4 Characteristics	6 Characteristics	None
Percentage rating	83%	83%	67%	67%	67%	100%	00%

Observe that only one of the references rates 100 percent—Revelation 10:7; 11:18. Only this one gives *all* the facts about the Rapture. One should not in any way look down on the others with ratings from 67 to 83 percent, because it would be artificial if every passage would give all the designations.

Not only did the mighty Messenger make a solemn oath about the time of the Rapture, but He also gave John a little scroll:

> Then the voice which I had heard speaking from heaven once more addressed me, saying, "Go and take the scroll

which lies open in the hand of the angel who is standing on the sea and on the land."

So I went to the angel and asked him to give me the small scroll.

"Take it," he said, "and eat the whole of it. It will give you great pain when you have eaten it, although in your mouth it will taste as sweet as honey."

So I took the small scroll out of the angel's hand and ate the whole of it; and in my mouth it was as sweet as honey, but when I had eaten it, it gave me great pain. And a voice said to me,

"You must prophesy yet further concerning peoples, nations, languages, and many kings." (10:8–11 WEYMOUTH)

This scroll contains the predictions which have not yet been revealed. Chewing of the scroll symbolizes careful study, digestion, and assimilation of God's Word, thus giving him the directives of the rest of the prophecy. Likewise, Ezekiel and Jeremiah developed rugged statures as great prophets because they ate scrolls of God's own making (Ezekiel 3:1–3; Jeremiah 15:16–18).

God's method of feeding and indoctrinating these three great prophets should make Christendom do a little thinking. Today many church members only eat the sterilized food products prepared by the human leaders. Such a method has both good and bad features.

To use another metaphor, the views of most believers conform exactly to the church mold in which they were cast. Is it not absurd for any member to claim that he has obtained his doctrines from eating God's Word alone, if he and all the other members are mouthing the exact creeds of that church?

How refreshingly different was God's schooling of the prophets! They chewed and digested God's unchangeable Word and then spoke it out—sometimes with fear but never with favor. No wonder there is such a unity to their messages, whereas there is a babel to the dogmas of man. I have said all of this to make this plea: Please, do not accept my or any other human interpretation of God's Word, until you have chewed and thoroughly digested that Holy Word with the help of the Holy Spirit (John 14:26; 16:13).

In my mouth it was as sweet as honey, but when I had eaten it, it gave me great pain. The gathering of God's saints to heaven, the handing out of glorious rewards, the marriage banquet of our Lord and the glories of the New Heavens and the New Earth—these were sweet as honey. But when John's stomach began to digest the full meaning of the bitter calamities "concerning peoples, nations, languages and many kings," John writhed with inner cramps.

But John, the loving disciple, was a true prophet. He recorded accurately God's message—the sweet with the bitter—the latter without any artificial sweeteners. May each of us prepare our hearts to accept both the bitter and the sweet in the chapters that follow!

13

TREATY—TEMPLE—TRICKSTER— TRIBULATION

Revelation 11

ISRAEL BUILDS HER TEMPLE! If that newspaper headline appeared today, hundreds of millions would be aroused. But someday the temple will be in Jerusalem, just as the Lord and the prophets predicted.

Does one have *factual* bases for believing Biblical prophecies? Let the record speak. Jesus predicted the capture of Jerusalem, the destruction of the temple and world-wide dispersion of the Jews (Matthew 24:2; Luke 21:24). Within forty years these three unusual predictions were literally fulfilled. These and other factual fulfillments in this century do give solid bases for believing that other prophecies will come to pass.

True, His prophecies about the regathering of the Jews, the rebirth of the nation and the recapture of Jerusalem did gather the sneers and the spittle of scoffers over the centuries. With the passing of so much time and the changing of circumstances, these predictions did appear bizarre. Suleiman the Magnificent, Sultan of the Ottoman Empire, rebuilt all around Jerusalem a massive and fantastically high stone wall (1542). The idea of a small and scattered Jewry regathering to become a nation and capturing this fortified city smacked of the ridiculous. Only God could do that!

But in this twentieth century a chain of miracles, like a chain of firecrackers, began to pop and made the world sit up and take notice. On May 14, 1948, the culmination of many miracles took place: *Israel became an independent nation.*

Ezekiel's valley of dry bones clacked together and began doing all sorts of remarkable feats (Ezekiel 37). Never had the world seen a nation destroyed, dispersed, so persecuted, and then become a nation after twenty-five hundred years! Israel was truly a *witness* of the veracity of God's Word.

Then that fledgling nation miraculously survived vicious attacks by numerically superior Arab nations in 1948, 1956, and 1967, not to mention severe harassment between these wars. In 1967 the world expected the invading Arab nations to carry out their publicly declared purpose to cast every Israeli into the sea, but another miracle of divine witnessing took place. Israel soundly routed these nations in the Six-Day War, the shortest war in modern history.

Israel also captured the Holy City, Jerusalem! On the Sunday following this capture, I attended a church service in Capetown, South Africa. A lay deacon stood up and said, "Brethren, permit me to read a prophecy of our Lord that has been fulfilled this past week," and he read Luke 21:24.

> And they shall fall by the edge of the sword, and shall be led away captive into all nations; and Jerusalem shall be trodden down of the Gentiles, until the times of the Gentiles be fulfilled. (KJV)

When Israel captured the Holy City in 1967, she obtained the ancient site of her temple. But on this site sits the great and very holy Dome of the Rock, often called the Mosque of Omar. The Mohammedans built it in A.D. 688. It is thirteen hundred years old and is as holy as it is old. If Israel would even whisper about razing this mosque, she would pull down on her little head the murderous wrath of 425 million Moslems. I discovered on this subject the Israeli keep their lips tightly zippered.

Will Israel ever be able to build her temple? Four prophets indicate that she will: Daniel (Daniel 9:27; Jesus (Matthew 24:15); Paul (2 Thessalonians 2:4) and John (Revelation 11:1,2).

Observe what Daniel writes:

> This king [Antichrist] will make a seven-year treaty with the people, but after half that time, he will break his pledge and stop the Jews from all their sacrifices and their offerings; then, as a climax to all his terrible deeds, the Enemy shall utterly defile the sanctuary of God. But in God's time and plan, His judgment will be poured out upon this Evil One. (Daniel 9:27 LP)

Here Daniel predicts *two* periods, each 3½ years long. The first is peaceful, but the second is full of tribulation. This very important verse can be summarized with four words that could profitably be memorized: Treaty—Temple—Trickster—Tribulation. The *king* is generally considered to be the Antichrist, hence my insertion of Antichrist in brackets. Perhaps Israel signs the treaty to get help to hold the Mohammedan world back, while she razes the mosque. John not only sees this temple but measures it:

> . . . And I was given a measuring rod like a staff, and I was told: "Get up and measure the Temple of God, and the altar, and count those who worship there. But leave out of your measurement the courtyard outside the Temple—do not measure that at all. For it has been given over to the nations, and they will trample over the holy city for forty-two months. (11:1,2 PHILLIPS)

Here the Apostle John is also describing the same two periods that Daniel predicted. Verse 1 gives 3½ years of tranquility and worship under the treaty but verse 2 indicates Israel's 3½ years of tribulation under the heel of the Antichrist.

God's Sanctuary (Greek *naos*). This Greek word does not refer to the entire temple, only to the holy inner chambers. Sanctuary is better and is given by some translators. Measurement here symbolizes and emphasizes the holiness of the sanctuary as elsewhere (Zechariah 2; Ezekiel 40; Revelation 21:15–17). The idea reminds one of a prospector who measures and stakes out a claim. This procedure publicizes and serves as a warning to trespassers.

Count the worshipers who are in it. The counting symbolizes God's appreciation of those Israeli who are putting God's interests ahead of personal pursuits. This may well be the group of Israeli whom God seals and protects (Revelation 7:1–8; 9:4; 12:6,13–16).

John next describes two witnesses:

> "And I will give authority to my two witnesses to proclaim the message, clothed in sackcloth for twelve hundred and sixty days."
> These are the two olive trees and the two lampstands which stand before the Lord of the earth. (11:3,4 PHILLIPS)

Who are these two witnesses? John states that they are the two olive trees "which stand before the Lord of the earth." How significantly similar to Zechariah's "two olive trees . . . that stand by the Lord of the whole earth" (Zechariah 4:11,14). God explained to Zechariah that these two olive trees were the "two anointed ones." Undoubtedly these were the two men anointed by God to rebuild Israel and the temple: Zerubbabel the governor and Jeshua the High Priest (Ezra 5:2). As the leaders of the nation these men, because of their dedicated work, made themselves and Israel a great witness to all the nations. They witnessed that Jehovah was not a god of wood and stone but One who was truly alive and active in restoring Israel, as His prophets predicted.

In the Revelation, John looks across the centuries to see the two olive trees' future counterparts of the two anointed men of old—Israel's leaders in the building of the temple. John's two witnesses may be Israel's future leaders who, by their work, will verify the predictions of the temple of the last days.

The "two olive trees"—Israel's leaders of the future—will have solid factual reasons to present Israel as a witness of God's miraculous care: her phenomenal regathering, the birth of the nation, the capture of Jerusalem, and the building of the temple. Such miraculous witnessing to God's power will not go unchallenged by the Arabs. Yet their harassment and warring activities will only give Israel further opportunity to witness to God's care.

> . . . If anyone tries to harm them, fire issues from their mouths and consumes their enemies. Indeed, if anyone should try to hurt them, this is the way in which he will certainly meet his death. These witnesses have power to shut up the sky and stop any rain from falling during the time of their preaching. Moreover, they have power to turn the waters into blood, and to strike the earth with any plague as often as they wish. (11:5,6 PHILLIPS)

Fire issues from their mouths and consumes their enemies. Probably not from the mouths of Israel's leaders but from the flame throwers of the army. Israel in defending herself has repeatedly used napalm and will not hesitate to use it again.

Power to shut up the sky and stop any rain. Until a few years ago, many thought such power had to be supernatural. But not now! Gordon J.F. MacDonald, associate director of the Institute of Geophysics and Planetary Physics at the University of California, Los Angeles writing under the title, "How to Wreck the Environment," in *Unless Peace Comes,* states that science is slowly bridging the gap between fact and fiction of the Jules Verne variety. Much research has in view weapons aimed at changing weather, climate, earthquakes, and tidal waves. Every one expects floods, hurricanes, drought, earthquakes, and tidal waves. Hence, one would be slow to suspect a nation being responsible. For this reason, any nation equipped with such weapons could produce apparently natural catastrophies in enemy territory without fear of any reprisal. Over a period of weeks or months it could ruin the entire economy. Before long the enemy would have little strike-back capability.

Most people know about the use of long-distance radio waves. But few know that scientists are now studying the use of brain waves to change the behavior of people. The Brain Research Institute of the University of California is enlarging man's knowledge in this field, reports MacDonald. Such a weapon if perfected would have devastating consequences in any war.

The strange feats described in Revelation 11:5,6 are not beyond the power of scientists to reproduce in the days ahead. Israeli scientists can be expected to be in the forefront in the discoveries of the future as the Jews have been in the past. Science, added to Israel's all-powerful motivation for survival, will continue to make Israel a witness that God is alive and fulfilling His promises to regather and to rebuild.

However, Israel's two leaders are only given 3½ years to witness after she makes a treaty with the Antichrist (Daniel 9:27; Revelation 11:3). And when this time is up the Antichrist breaks the treaty and kills Israel's leaders and witness. The following verses give the details:

> ... But when they have completed their testimony, the beast that comes up from the abyss will wage war upon them and will defeat and kill them. Their corpses will lie in the street of the great city, whose name in allegory is Sodom, or Egypt, where also their Lord was crucified. For three days and a half men from every people and tribe, of every language and nation, gaze upon their corpses and refuse them burial. All men on earth gloat over them, make merry, and exchange presents; for these two prophets were a torment to the whole earth. (11:7–10 NEB)

The emergence of the Antichrist in his true role marks the beginning of Israel's greatest tribulation (Matthew 24:16,21). This distress will also last 3½ years (Revelation 13:5). This period of 3½ *years* may be symbolized by the 3½ *days* above when Israel's two witnesses will be silenced.

How can the people of every nation gaze upon the corpses of these two witnesses in Jerusalem? Such a prediction was absurd until the advent of television. And it was impossible until the United States put a satellite in outer space from which to bounce TV impulses. Some of my respected intellectual friends may part company from me, in view of such statements. They will also have to part company with that outstanding scholar Dr. John F. Walvoord, President of Dallas Theological Seminary. I am indebted to him for his interpretation here of television as set forth in *The Revelation of Jesus Christ.*

All-men on earth gloat over them. Every Arab nation will declare a national holiday. Every Communist will rejoice that God's chosen people have been soundly defeated. Every atheist will rejoice because Israel's defeat proves that God is dead. And many Christians who only have superficial knowledge of future events will think that God's prophets made a mistake in talking about Israel's future.

But the gloating of the Antichrist, Arabs, and atheists will be short-lived. As in Belshazzar's feast, their celebration over the fall of Israel will have a sudden surprising finale.

> But at the end of the three days and a half the breath of life from God came into them; and they stood up on their feet to the terror of all who saw it. Then a loud voice was heard speaking to them from heaven, which said, "Come up here!" And they went up to heaven in a cloud, in full view of their enemies. At that same moment there was a violent earthquake, and a tenth of the city fell. Seven thousand people were killed in the earthquake; the rest in terror did homage to the God of heaven.
>
> The second woe has now passed. But the third is soon to come. (11:11–14 NEB)

And they went up to heaven . . . in full view of their enemies. Since the resurrection of the two witnesses was visible to the world, one wonders if the Rapture of the church may not be visible, too. Terrorized by the supernatural resurrection and ascension of the witnesses and by the earthquake, "the rest did homage to the God of heaven." It took the resurrection and the ascension of the witnesses to convince the people that God was truly working in the leaders of Israel.

The second woe, the sixth trumpet, which began in Revelation 9:13 is now over. The third woe, soon to come, is the seventh or last trumpet. How soon before God's wrath is poured out on a wicked world, no one is told. But when the seventh angel is about to sound the last trump, the righteous dead and living rise to meet. In the verses that follow in Revelation 11, one observes that the Rapture is clearly pre-wrath. The Church will surely escape the wrath of God. Note the events that occur before this wrath is poured out.

Then the seventh angel blew his trumpet; and voices were heard in heaven shouting:

'The sovereignty of the world has passed to our Lord and his Christ, and he shall reign for ever and ever!'

And the twenty-four elders, seated on their thrones before God, fell on their faces and worshipped God, saying:

'We give thee thanks, O Lord God, sovereign over all, who art and who wast, because thou hast taken thy great power into thy hands and entered upon thy reign. The nations raged, but thy day of retribution has come. Now is the time for the dead to be judged; now is the time for recompense to thy servants the prophets, to thy dedicated people, and all who honour thy name, both great and small, the time to destroy those who destroy the earth.' (11:15–18 NEB)

Now is the time for the dead to be judged. These are the righteous dead. Here the righteous dead are judged and rewarded according to their deeds (1 Corinthians 3:13–15). The wicked dead are not raised until the thousand years of the Millennium are over (Revelation 20:5).

Only *after the seventh trumpet sounds,* do the elders note that it is now the time for three great events to take place:

1 The Lord God begins His reign on the earth.
2 The saints are judged and rewarded.
3 The living wicked are destroyed.

The fact that the saints are not judged and rewarded until the seventh trumpet sounds, confirms the viewpoint that the Rapture must have occurred when the last trump began to sound (Revelation 10:7). That view makes a logical time interval between the resurrection of the saints and their rewarding. A seven-year interval between these two events, as some teach, is definitely unreasonable.

Recompense to thy dedicated people both great and small. Not social status but dedication to the Lord determines the measure of the reward. Paul states that God's fire will also test the worth of every man's work. Pathetic it will be for those Christians who devote their time in this life building things with "hay and stubble." But glorious will be the special rewards of those who build with "gold and silver" (1 Corinthians 3:12–15).

Finally, the details of God's wrath are given:

> Then God's temple in heaven was laid open, and within the temple was seen the ark of his covenant. There came flashes of lightning and peals of thunder, and earthquake, and a storm of hail. (Revelation 11:19 NEB)

Here is the description of the last day of this age. It is called the Day of God's Wrath. See chart in chapter 24.

14

ISRAEL—GOD'S SIGN IN THE SKY

Revelation 12:1–5

In June, 1968, the world was shocked by the assassination of Senator Robert Kennedy by an Arab. In the pocket of the assassin were clippings of Senator Kennedy's speeches, favoring United States aid to Israel. At his trial he confessed he killed the senator because of these views.

This murder is only a small facet of a struggle that began 4,000 years ago between Abraham's sons, Isaac and Ishmael. From Isaac came the Jews while from Ishmael came the Arabs. Since the United States is lined up with Israel and Russia is behind the Arab nations, this ancient family feud now has global impact.

The Middle East is the hub of three continents: Europe, Africa, and Asia. Here is the Suez Canal, the important waterway linking these vast and populous areas. Last and most important here is 60 percent of the world's oil supply.

Hence, any event here commands the attention of the world. Yet the world today can neither understand in depth what is happening here nor see what is ahead. Today man has his satellites to tell him if it is going to rain but he can't discern the "signs of the times." He fails to see the great sign that God has placed in the sky to help him understand the events of the world. The following verse presents this sign:

Then a huge sign became visible in the sky—the figure of a woman clothed with the sun, with the moon under her feet and a crown of twelve stars upon her head. She was pregnant, and cried out in her labor and in the pains of bringing forth her child. (Revelation 12:1,2 PHILLIPS)

In Genesis 37:9, the sun and moon represent Joseph's father and mother, while twelve stars stand for the twelve sons, the ancestors of the twelve tribes of Israel. Clearly the woman in Revelation 12:1 is Israel. For many centuries Israel has been God's sign in the sky for all the world to see. Both in her successes and failures, Israel has ever been a sign to prove the veracity of God's predictive Word. (See *Guide*, Appendix 29.)

Next John sees a second sign, this one terrifying:

Then another sign became visible in the sky, and I saw that it was a huge red dragon with seven heads and ten horns, with a diadem upon each of its heads. His tail swept down a third of the stars in the sky and hurled them upon the earth. The dragon took his place in front of the woman who was about to give birth to a child, so that as soon as she did so he might devour it. She gave birth to a male child who is to shepherd all the nations "with a rod of iron." Her child was snatched up to God and to his throne. (12:3–5 PHILLIPS)

This dragon is clearly labeled as "the devil and Satan." (12:9). The woman's son who will shepherd all nations "with a rod of iron" is identified as Christ (Psalm 2:9; Revelation 19:15). This latter statement confirms the view that the woman is Israel, the nation of our Lord.

Here are two great signs in the sky of the world—Israel and her enemy Satan. Satan has a special hatred for Israel because he knows that she will produce the Messiah destined to bruise his head (Genesis 3:15). His many attempts through the centuries to murder all those in the Messianic line make him a *sign*. He instigated Pharoah to kill all Hebrew baby boys at birth. He incited Athaliah to kill her own grandsons, in his fiendish attempts to wipe out the Messianic line.

Then there was Haman who had a grudge against one insignificant Jew. (Esther 3). Satan seems to have been involved in Haman's getting a decree to kill every Jew in the Persian Empire.

At the time of Jesus' birth, "the Dragon took his place" to devour the babe. Satan capitalized on Herod's jealousy to slay every babe under two years in the vicinity of Bethlehem.

It was Satan who tried to kill Jesus during the time of the temptation. One also reads that Satan entered into Judas who then betrayed Jesus to be crucified (Luke 22:3). Through the centuries there has been a Satanic element in the frightful persecutions of the Jews. In this enlightened century it is difficult to imagine a nation as cultured as Germany massacring nearly 6 million men, women, and children without its being incited by a fiendish devilish agent. That vast *purposeless* slaughter stemmed from a deeply seated hate—utterly inhuman.

Before the Lord was crucified, His disciples asked Him for signs that would point to the destruction of the temple and to His return to this earth. Jesus pointed to a sign that was in the sky then and still is today —Israel, the nation and its Jerusalem.

Observe the signs that Jesus gave and the accurate fulfillment of His predictions. The disciples wanted to know what sign would forewarn them of the time of the destruction of the temple and Jerusalem. He told them that when Jerusalem would be surrounded by hostile armies, that would be the *sign* for them to flee.

In less than forty years Titus beseiged and captured Jerusalem. He destroyed the temple and killed one million Jews. Eusebius states that Christians fled and thus saved their lives, probably as a result of heeding Jesus' advice to flee (Luke 21:20,21).

Jesus also predicted that the Jews would be killed, dispersed "among all nations," and severely persecuted. In their world-wide dispersion and horrible persecutions, the Jews have been a most remarkable *sign* of the veracity of God's predictive Word. A sign in the sky that all the world has seen for nineteen centuries!

When Titus captured Jerusalem (A.D. 70), he was ruthless. Josephus states he killed 1,100,000. In A.D. 132 Hadrian killed thousands more. Then the Romans scoured the land to kill every Jew. Any Jew found in Jerusalem was promptly killed. As the Jews wandered over the earth, almost everywhere they were cursed, spit upon, stoned, and killed. In any country where plague or calamity hit, the poor Jew was blamed and severely persecuted.

Hence, with the passing of centuries, a few straggled back to Palestine. But as late as 1882 there were only twenty-four thousand Jews in their former homeland. The modern return began in 1882 after a savage pogrom in Russia (*pogrom* is a Russian word meaning "devastation"). At that time seven thousand returned. But they couldn't survive because of the dry rocky ground, the hostile Turkish police, and the marauding bands of Arabs. Many died and others left.

In 1897 Theodor Herzl, a brilliant journalist, called the first Zionist

Congress to Switzerland. Two hundred delegates from all over the world were electrified by Herzl's preposterous proposal—the rebirth of a free and independent Israel.

In 1903 another massacre of Jews was launched in Russia. As a result thirty thousand Russian and Polish Jews sailed for Palestine. Ben Gurion was one of these. These Jews had fought for their lives against Russian Cossacks and Polish hooligans. They were better conditioned to tangle with the Turks and Arabs in Palestine.

Yet, God was working too "in a mysterious way His wonders to perform." Chaim Weizmann, a Russian Jew, had emigrated to England. He studied and became a brilliant scientist. At that time England was losing World War 1, one reason being her lack of acetone, needed to make smokeless gunpowder. She then implored Weizmann to design an easy way to make the precious acetone. In less than a month he devised an ingenious technique.

A grateful Lloyd George recommended him to the King for any honors that Weizmann might name.

"I want nothing for myself," said Weizmann. "All I desire is a homeland for my people."

As a result England publicized the *Balfour Declaration* (November 2, 1917). This document promised England's backing to establish a Jewish homeland in Palestine.

God must have been working too—months later General Edmund H. Allenby wrested Palestine from Turkey (1918). Then the League of Nations not only gave the Mandate of Palestine to England but in that Mandate she also incorporated the spirit of the Balfour Declaration— the rebirth of Israel as an independent nation.

These favorable episodes zoomed Jewish immigration. The Jews bought useless marshes from the Arabs and drained these. Agriculture began to flourish. Then jealousy caused the Arabs to object to Jewish immigration. Because England had vast oil interests in Iran and Iraq, she yielded to the Arabs and drastically restricted Jewish immigration and purchases of all lands.

In fact, England issued a White Paper (1939) limiting immigration to fifteen thousand a year for five years when it was to stop entirely. Thus England reneged not only on her Balfour Declaration but also on the Mandate from the League of Nations.

England's White Paper was a death warrant. It welded the doors shut for the countless thousands trying to escape from Hitler's crematories. Like caged rats, Jewish men, women, and children scurried to save their lives. Irving Miller, in *Israel, the Eternal Ideal*, describes the plight of the Jews:

101

Soon afterward there followed the horror of the "floating coffins." Jews fleeing from the tortures of the concentration camps and the crematoria of Hitler, packed themselves in the filthy holds of tramp steamers, oversized tugboats, anything their friends could beg or buy and set sail for freedom in Palestine. These pitiful craft were intercepted by British naval vessels and forced back to their point of origin in Hitler's Europe. Protesting, the refugees were dragged from the holds, then interned in detention camps.

(If one can stomach another glimpse of the history of that day, see *Guide,* Appendix 31.)

After the stench of Hitler's crematories blew away, the outlook for a Jewish nation was indeed bleak. In 1945 the Jews in Palestine numbered only 521,564. These were the targets of about one million Palestinian Arabs. The years 1946–48 were terror years. The Jews, knowing there was no other place to go, fought fiercely for survival. The Arabs were determined to exterminate them and confiscate the farms that they had made. Palestine became a bloody battlefield.

Finally, the United Nations divided Palestine between the Jews and the Arabs. But the Arabs would not agree to give the Jews *any* land. However, the United Nations voted that this partition would go into effect on May 14, 1948.

On that date England moved the last of its peace-keeping forces out. On that day the armies of Lebanon, Syria, Jordan, Iraq, and Egypt moved in for the kill. Their purpose was mouthed by Azzam Pasha, Secretary General of the Arab League, "This will be a war of extermination and a momentous massacre."

The goal seemed certain of attainment. According to J. Bowyer Bell in *The Long War* the Arabs could recruit from 40 million. Historian Cecil Roth gives the Jewish population as only 655,000. There were sixty-one Arabs to one Jew. Five Goliaths defiantly strode toward one youngster equipped with a sling shot, so to speak. Israel had neither a proper army nor an air force. And the United Nations, the white horse rider, had nary an arrow to enforce its paper partition (Revelation 6:1,2).

Egypt began by bombing Tel Aviv. The armies of Lebanon and Syria swarmed in from the north. The famous Arab Legion moved toward the Jewish city of Jerusalem. Here lived one hundred thousand Jews who were completely encircled except for one narrow road to Tel Aviv. Their starvation or slaughter seemed certain.

But these Israelis, their wives, and little ones, facing certain annihilation, fought furiously. To keep the food line open to Tel Aviv, old men, boys, and girls fought fiercely and many died.

It was a miracle that the UN ever voted to make Israel an independent nation. The nation was born May 14, 1948. It was a second miracle that the newborn nation was able to defeat the five nations that attacked her.

Although large-scale fighting stopped, yet Arab gangs continued to harass Israel with terror raids, sniping, and bombing. Egypt, too, kept up her unprovoked attacks. Then Israel in a brilliant military maneuver captured the entire Sinai Peninsula (1956). However, Israel withdrew because of pressure from the UN and a promise from President Dwight D. Eisenhower that Israel's gateway to the south would always be international waters.

When 1967 came, Russia had again trained and replenished the Arabs with the latest in planes, tanks—a total of two billion dollars worth of military hardware. Nasser boasted that "our basic aim is the destruction of Israel." Nasser moved eighty thousand troops along Israel's southern border, while Russia blocked every attempt in the UN to avert war. Egypt ordered the "peace-keeping" troops of the UN stationed on the Egyptian-Israeli border to pull out (May 18). The U.N.'s white horse (Revelation 6:1,2) never made a whine. The powerless nag threw its tail back and made a world-record getaway. *Twelve* Arab nations promised Nasser full support.

Two days later Nasser closed Israel's lifeline to the south—the Gulf of Aqaba—which President Eisenhower had promised would be international waters. If Israel had assumed such a warlike stance against any of her neighbors the UN would have promptly threatened Israel with sanctions or worse. But with Russia dominant in the UN, the peace-loving white horse, continued to eat her oats in her New York City stable as an international volcano readied to erupt. U Thant calmly announced on May 27 that "the outbreak of hostilities is at hand."

Hero of the 1956 Sinai campaign, one-eyed Dayan had charge of the Israeli forces. He did not dare wait until Israel's oil was depleted. His only sensible defense was an attack! This he did on Monday June 5, 1967.

That morning Russian Kosygin used the hot line between Moscow and Washington—the first time since its installation four years before. It was reported that Kosygin awakened President Johnson at 4:30 A.M. to tell him that Israel and Egypt were at war. He promised Johnson that Russia would not interfere if the United States stayed out. Johnson agreed.

On the first day of the war, in less than three hours, Israel destroyed

300 of Egypt's 340 air force planes. A miracle! The huge mechanized Egyptian army became a fleeing rabble.

Israel churned through the Sinai deserts and reached the Suez Canal on Wednesday. Egypt fearing for Cairo signed a cease fire on the fourth day of the war.

On the eastern front the Jordanian air force was smashed. The Jordanians, the best troops in the Arab world, were taken apart on the second day of the war.

After the miraculous defeats of Egypt and Jordan, Israel paused before attacking Syria. This nation had harassed Israel incessantly for years. When Russia saw the phenomenal success of Israel against Egypt and Jordan, she sought to protect her Syrian ally. She introduced a resolution in the UN calling for a cease fire. In a few more days Syria bowed. In only six days Israel had squelched the armies of the Arab nations! They also took the great bulge west of the Jordan. Also captured was the entire Sinai Peninsula with one bank of the Suez Canal.

Repeatedly I heard of people in Israel saying, "Before the Six-Day War I was an atheist. I didn't believe in anything. But after I saw the miracles of that war, I had to believe in God."

In the spectacular victories of 1948, 1956, and 1967, Israel, the woman crowned with twelve stars, was a *sign* to all the world that God was alive and verifying His prophetic Word.

To His surprised disciples Jesus predicted the capture of Jerusalem, the utter destruction of the temple, and the dispersion of the Jews. He gave them signs regarding the time of the fulfillment (Matthew 24:1,2; Luke 21:20). These were all fulfilled within a few years.

They also asked Him for a *sign* of His return to this earth and the end of this age (Matthew 24:3). He then gave them quite a few signs, most of them related to Israel (24:4–34). Most of them have been and are being fulfilled in the middle of our twentieth century.

He predicted the frightful persecution of the Jews, the regathering, the rebirth of the nation, and the recapture of Jerusalem.

He stated that when the fig tree (Israel) began to bud again, His return would be near: ". . . you may know that he is near, at your very door!" (Matthew 24:33 PHILLIPS). Because Satan also knows that the rebirth of Israel means the return soon of Christ and Satan's punishment, one can see clearly why Satan has been seeking to kill every Jew and to destroy the nation of Israel. He must thwart Israel and God's plan or he will be destroyed. (See fig tree, *Guide,* Appendix 30.)

How thrilling and exciting to be alive in this century! Almost nightly the headlines of newspapers refer to the struggle going on between God's two signs in the sky—the woman (Israel) and that old serpent, the Devil!

15

WHAT'S NEXT IN THE MIDDLE EAST?

Revelation 12:6–17

Because events in the Middle East have global impact, world leaders are keeping an anxious eye on this barrel of dynamite. They are trying to see its future in order to save their countries from threatening involvement and catastrophe.

What's next in the Middle East? Look at this problem first from a purely human viewpoint. The trouble really stems from Russia's desire to dominate this strategic area holding 60 percent of the world's oil supply. Russia is merely using the Arab nations as puppets. This nation has been and still is the poorly hidden agent who pulls all the strings and mouths all the propaganda.

Israel won the miraculous victory in 1967 because the war was over in six days, before slow Russia shifted into gear. But in this decade of the 1970s the outlook for Israel is not bleak but black. With all nations giving increasing subservience to the Soviet Union, Israel doesn't need *any* fingers to count her friends. These so-called friends are recently only concerned with their own interests.

For years Russia has vetoed every proposal in the United Nations that was favorable to Israel and against the Arabs. France not only refused to deliver planes promised to Israel but pocketed all the money paid. England, hurting for lack of export business, now refuses to sell any tanks to Israel. West Germany, another good friend of Israel in the past, elected in the late 1969 a leader who began a courtship with Moscow and neighboring communistic nations.

Last and most important, Nixon's Secretary of State William Rogers announced that Israel should give back the territory that she took in 1967. In return the Arab nations are to promise to be nice to Israel in the future. Israel is not naïve enough to accept such a pledge from a people who have repeatedly and publicly announced that there can be no peace in the Middle East until every Israeli is cast into the sea. For Israel to give back these strategic military areas at a time when she is devoid of friends would be to commit suicide.

In the Middle East, the United States has recently shifted into neutral gear. Reason? Billions of dollars in Arabian oil!

That is the dismal outlook as man looks at the situation. Now take the guesswork out of human forecasts and look at the Middle East through the eyes of God's prophets. No one should doubt their reliability after seeing the remarkable fulfillment of three of their prophecies in this twentieth century:

1 Long awaited regathering of the Jews to Palestine (Ezekiel 37).
2 Rebirth of Israel as a nation (Matthew 24:32,33). (See *Guide*, Appendix 30.)
3 The capture of Jerusalem (Luke 21:24).

At the beginning of this century all three of these prophecies looked impossible. Yet all came to pass in spite of the devil, Hitler's crematories, and Arab hate.

In view of these remarkable fulfillments, every person, Christian or atheist, should now look with confidence to see what the Bible predicts next. Refer again to the Book of Daniel:

> This king [the Antichrist] will make a seven-year treaty with the people [the Israelis], but after half that time, he will break his pledge and stop the Jews from all their sacrifices and their offerings; then, as a climax to all his terrible deeds, the Enemy shall utterly defile the sanctuary of God. But in God's time and plan, His judgment will be poured out upon this Evil One. (9:27 LP)

Observe the nuggets of information in this passage.

This king. Many scholars believe that he is the Antichrist.

Seven-year treaty. This is the last of seventy periods of seven years, a total of 490 years. In this last seven years God completes all of His dealings with Israel as a distinct people (Daniel 9:24). Observe and remember that this last seven-year period *begins* with a treaty with the Antichrist. It will end with their acceptance of Christ (Ezekiel 39:28; Zechariah 12:10; 14:9).

He will break his pledge. Three and a half years after the Antichrist makes a treaty with Israel, he will break it. He stops the Israelis from worshiping in their temple. This will cause a great furor among the orthodox and many of these will pay with their lives for refusing to conform (Revelation 13:15).

Shall utterly defile the sanctuary of God. He does this by placing his image in the Holy of Holies (Matthew 24:15; 2 Thessalonians 2:4; Revelation 13:15). Anybody who does not worship this abominable image will be promptly killed. All over Israel there will be a terrible slaughter.

Fortunately, the Lord gives directions how they can escape this slaughter, the greatest tribulation of all time (Matthew 24:21). Every Israeli should memorize this life-saving passage:

> When therefore ye see the abomination of desolation, which was spoken of through Daniel the prophet, standing in the holy place . . . let them that are in Judea flee unto the mountains. . . . (Matthew 24:15,16 ASV)

Some of the believing Israelis will do just that and John gives some detail about it:

> The woman fled into the wilderness, where God had prepared a place for her, to take care of her for 1260 days. (Revelation 12:6 LNT)

To take care of her for 1260 days (3½ years). For the first three and one-half years , when the Antichrist permits the Israelis to worship in their temple, there is comparative tranquility and peace in Israel. But the setting up of the image in the holy place marks the end of 3½ years of peace and introduces another 3½ years (1260 days). This 3½ years is one of terror—the Great Tribulation. (See *Guide,* Appendix 32 for vital background summary of this three and one-half years.)

Who are the Israelis who flee? They could well be the 144,000 sealed *just before* the Tribulation and the blowing of the trumpets began (Revelation 7:1-3). Because they had fled out of the country, they did not suffer from the tortures of this period (9:1-5).

Where will these Israelis flee? Jesus said the "mountains" while John referred to "the wilderness." Since mountains in Israel are arid wildernesses there is no contradiction here. But which mountains, for the whole area abounds with mountainous deserts?

For many years scholars have suggested that no mountain offers the protection from a foe to equal that of the ancient city of Petra. Centuries ago this was the capital of the Nabataeans. Still in existence are the huge buildings, with great rooms and chambers, carved out of solid pink rock. These would offer wonderful protection from even nuclear bombs. This fantastic city can only be reached by a very narrow road easily defended by a handful of people.

No one can be sure if this will be the haven that God has prepared for the Israelis. The Lord might use this very likely place or prepare a better one with one of His earthquakes.

Daniel also states that when the Antichrist invades "the fair land of Palestine" he will overthrow many nations but "Moab, Edom, and most of Ammon will escape" (Daniel 11:41 LNT). Petra is situated in Edom, south of the Dead Sea.

The Israelis who fail to heed Jesus' admonition to flee will suffer frightfully. Zechariah predicts that two-thirds will be killed while the suffering of the remaining third is likened to the white hot fire that refines silver (Zechariah 13:8,9).

Satan must have inspired Hitler to commit the crimes that he did. Likewise, the spirit of the devil within the Antichrist will drive him to scourge and torture the Israelis far beyond anything in their awful past. In the verses that follow, the Bible gives the reason for this frightening increase of Satanic hate:

Then war broke out in Heaven. Michael and his angels battled with the dragon. The dragon and his angels fought back, but they did not prevail and they were expelled from Heaven. So the huge dragon, the serpent of ancient times, who is called the devil and Satan, the deceiver of the whole world, was hurled down upon the earth, and his angels were hurled down with him. (Revelation 12:7–9 PHILLIPS)

Then war broke out in Heaven. This war and the complete expulsion of Satan from heaven is still in the future. (See *Guide,* Appendix 21 for details.) When Satan and his angels are wholly excluded from heaven there will be great rejoicing:

Then I heard a loud voice shouting across the heavens, "It has happened at last! God's salvation and the power and the rule, and the authority of His Christ are finally here; for the Accuser of our brothers has been thrown down from heaven onto earth—he accused them day and night before our God. (12:10 LNT)

His descent to the earth with all of his demons will bring added stress to Christians on the earth. But the heavenly voice gives three attitudes that will be helpful in liquidating the effect of Satan's impact:

They defeated him by the blood of the Lamb, and by their testimony; for they did not love their lives but laid them down for Him. (12:11 LNT)

Theirs was not freedom *from* persecution but the spirit of the unconquerable Paul who exaltingly said, "O Death, where is thy sting? O grave, where is thy victory?" A Christian must decide whether he will be a man or a mouse.

At the present time, Satan must have access to a fairly high plane in heaven as his expulsion gives joy and blessed relief to those in heaven. But it will mean great sorrow to those on the earth:

> Rejoice, oh heavens! you citizens of heaven, rejoice! be glad! But woe to you people of the world, for the devil has come down to you in great anger, knowing that he has little time. (12:12 LNT)

Satan knows prophesy. He knows he only has 3½ years before his punishment. Hence, with all of his demons now concentrated on the earth, he will devastate it and the people as he never did before. Alas for the earth! He will compensate for the brevity of time with ferocity of action.

This period is that of the Great Tribulation, the time of the blowing of the first six trumpets, the season of suffering for Israel, never before equalled in history (Matthew 24:21). But some of the Israelis will heed Jesus' advice to flee and they will be protected during the 3½ years of the Great Tribulation:

> And when the dragon saw that he had been cast down upon the earth, he began to pursue the woman who had given birth to the male child. But she was given two great eagle's wings so that she could fly to her place in the desert, where she is kept safe from the serpent for a time and times and half a time [3½ years]. (12:13,14 PHILLIPS)

The wings may be used here as a symbol of God's protective care, as in Exodus 19:4 and Deuteronomy 32:11,12. The mention of *two great eagle's wings* suggests the possibility of airplanes.

The old dragon was furious when he saw some of the Israelis escaping. He made an unusual effort to kill them:

> Then the serpent ejected water from his mouth, streaming like a river in pursuit of the woman, to drown her in its flood. But the earth came to the woman's rescue, opened its mouth and swallowed up the river which the dragon had emitted from his mouth. (12:15,16 PHILLIPS)

It is not necessary to decide whether this will be a literal or symbolic deliverance. Israel will probably build large dams in the Jordan River valley. Opening these to the full could create a deadly flood.

The earth swallowed up the river. Such language favors a literal interpretation. The drying up of the flood could be either natural or supernatural or both.

Satan, thus foiled and frustrated, vents his rage on everybody associated with Israel:

> Then the furious Dragon set out to attack the rest of her children—all who were keeping God's commandments and confessing that they belong to Jesus. (12:17 LNT)

Attack the rest of her children. That would include the Israelis remaining in Israel and the Jews scattered over the world. Satan also will attack Christians who "belong to Jesus."

The thrust of this verse is both anti-Jew and anti-Christian. Likewise, it is significant that from the days of its founder Karl Marx, communism has ever had a fiendish compulsion to destroy every trace of both Judaism and Christianity.

When Satan is finally cast out of heaven upon this earth, he will not need to look far for a people to do the deeds predicted in 12:17. The next chapter describes the dictator of that people, through whom Satan will work.

16

DANIEL'S PORTRAIT OF THE ANTICHRIST

(Preface to Revelation 13)

The greatest man that God produced was Jesus Christ. The most infamous character that Satan will energize is the Antichrist.

In the days ahead he will play the leading role in the affairs of this world. Nobody can buy or sell without his stamp. He will domineer "over all kindreds and tongues and nations" (Revelation 13:7 KJV). Everybody must worship as he dictates or else.

No human being should be studied more carefully! Yet most people know *nothing* about his many Scriptural portrayals. If one had only the portrait sketched by Daniel, he could readily recognize him.

While a captive in Babylon, Daniel had several visions of the last days of our age. Nebuchadnezzar, king of Babylon, had a distressing dream but he could not remember it. Daniel not only told him what his dream was but he interpreted it.

Daniel informed the king that he had seen a huge statue made of different metals. He told the king that he was the head of gold. The chest and the two arms of silver represented the next empire, Medo-Persia. The abdomen of brass typified the next kingdom in history, Greece. The iron thighs and legs were symbolical of the Roman Empire. The two legs stood for the eastern and western divisions of that empire (A.D. 395).

Thus Daniel saw these four great empires covering a span of one thousand years. So accurately were these predictions fulfilled that atheists, such as the Greek Pythagoras (who died about 497 B.C.), said that Daniel's predictions must have been written after Medo-Persia conquered Babylon. One should thank this Greek philosopher because his criticism was made long *before* Greece conquered Medo-Persia. (For more proof of the early date of Daniel's prophecy see *Guide*, Appendix 33.)

It has been many centuries since the ancient empires of Babylon, Medo-Persia, Greece, and Rome passed away, but Daniel's view of the empire symbolized by the ten toes of the image is still future in our day. These ten toes represent ten kings of kingdoms in existence when Christ will return to this earth. Daniel not only saw these ten kingdoms but as he looked he saw the great Stone (Christ), "cut from the mountain without human hands" (LP), fall down upon the ten wicked kingdoms and pulverize the whole image made of clay, iron, brass, silver and gold (Daniel 2:45).

Some years later Daniel saw these same kingdoms—now represented by wild beasts. He saw Babylon as a lion, Medo-Persia as a bear, Greece as a leopard, and the Roman Empire as a bizarre beast much more terrible than the others (Daniel 7).

The ten-toe kingdom, he now sees as ten horns on the last strange beast. Then as he looked, he saw another special horn arise in the midst of the ten horns. Here is something new that he didn't see in the first vision. The context of the following passage indicates that this unusual horn or King is the Antichrist:

> For out of its ten horns shall arise ten kings and after them shall
> arise another, who shall be different from the former kings,

and shall put down three of them. (Daniel 7:24 BERKELEY)
He will defy the Most High God, and wear down the saints
with persecution, and try to change all laws, morals and customs. God's people will be helpless in his hands for 3½ years.
(7:25 LP)

Ten kings will arise. Ten kings or kingdoms will arise out of the
territory formerly occupied by the Roman Empire. It is thrilling that
John also gives important facts about ten kings or kingdoms, whom he
closely associates with Rome, the capital of the Roman Empire (Revelation 17:12–17).

*Another king shall arise, who shall be different from the former
kings.* God now turns the spotlight on this distinctly different kind of
king. The kingdom that produces the Antichrist is different from anything that history ever produced in the past. What nation, what
ideology arose in this century that is outstandingly different from anything in the past?

He shall put down three of them. Not only is this nation radically
different in its ideology but it destroyed three of the ten nations and
must have made the other nations shake in their boots. Daniel tries to
impress the reader that this new nation is nihilistic. He is not content
with peaceful coexistence. His design is to liquidate other nations.
What nation today fits this description?

*He will defy the Most High God, and wear down the saints with
persecution.* A distinguishing mark of the Antichrist is his blatant defiance of God. With his blasphemy goes a murderous obsession to
persecute and kill God's followers. For what nation is this description
exactly tailored?

He will try to change all laws, morals and customs. In the 1960s half
a dozen well-organized militant groups had one radical common plan
—the destruction of "all laws, morals and customs." Their sole purpose
was to destroy the entire Establishment, strut over the wreckage of
Christian civilization, and decide at a later date how to rebuild it.

Drug use, pornography, nudity, sexual promiscuity, homosexuality,
rioting, violence, arson, bombing, and terrorism were glorified. Responsible agencies of the United States government examined these
activists groups in depth and then turned them bottom side up. Invariably they found the label FOR EXPORT USE ONLY. MADE IN RUSSIA!

God's people will be helpless in his hand 3½ years. It is helpful to
remember that the Great Tribulation will come to a glorious end—the
return of Christ. Repeatedly Daniel and John give this 3½ year interval, another illustration of the unity and inspiration of the Bible.

In the eighth chapter of Daniel, one obtains a more definitive picture of the Antichrist. This chapter describes a fierce battle between a ram (Medo-Persia) and a one-horned goat (Greece). This "great horn that is between his eyes is the first king" of Greece (8:21 KJV). Clearly, history declares this notable horn was Alexander the Great. (For a thrilling link between history and Daniel's prophecy see *Guide*, Appendix 34.)

When Greece vanquished Persia, Alexander became powerful, "but suddenly at the height of his power, his horn was broken; and in its place grew four good-sized horns" (8:8 LP).

History records that when Alexander died at an early age, his generals quarreled over his great empire. When the smoke of their battles cleared, four horns were seen:

1 Seleucus controlled the vast Syrian Empire reaching from Turkey to India. His empire was far greater than any of the others.
2 Ptolemy possessed Egypt.
3 Lysimachus held Thrace.
4 Cassander dominated Macedonia and Greece.

(*Guide*, Appendix 35 gives details about how this settlement took place.)

Then as Daniel looked at these four horns or kingdoms, he saw an arresting sight:

And out of one of them came forth a little horn. (8:9 ASV)

He even challenged the Commander of the army of heaven by canceling the daily sacrifices offered to Him, and by defiling His temple. (8:10,11 LP)

Out of one of the four horns came forth a little horn. The context in Daniel and history agree that this little horn was Antiochus Epiphanes (175–163 B.C.), one of the rulers of the great Seleucid or Syrian Empire. Learning that Egypt was preparing for war, Antiochus beat Ptolemy Philometor to the draw and took nearly all of the Delta region except Alexandria. The character of Antiochus is revealed in the blasphemous surname that he took—*Epiphanes, God in visible form.* Not only did he invade "the glorious land," Israel, but he had an obsession to eradicate every vestige of God in Israel. He robbed the temple of its sacred symbols and made the worship of himself mandatory. On the sacred altar he sacrificed a sow, abomination of all abominations. All sacred books were burned, circumcision was punishable by death, and those who observed the Sabbath Day were killed. (There are a number of excellent reference books on Bible land history and geography. *See* bibliography.)

On a trip back from conquering Ptolemy VI of Egypt, he attacked Jerusalem where it is said, he slew eighty thousand, took forty thousand, and sold forty thousand Jews into captivity.

Antiochus's persecution of the Jews covered 3½ years (spring of 168 B.C. to fall of 165 B.C.). Repeatedly Daniel and John give 3½ years as the duration of the Great Tribulation by the Antichrist. Was the Syrian emperor Antiochus the Antichrist?

Definitely not! He lived many centuries before the time that Gabriel told Daniel the Antichrist would appear:

> ". . . Son of man," he said, "you must understand that the events you have seen in your vision will not take place until the end times come." (Daniel 8:17 LP)

> "I am here," he said, "to tell you what is going to happen in the last days of the coming time of terror—for what you have seen pertains to that final event in history." (v.19)

Speaking of this Great Tribulation, "greater than any previous suffering in Jewish history" (12:1 LP), Daniel three times definitely gives the time as the "time of the end" or "those last days" (12:4,9,13).

Furthermore, Jesus, Paul, and John, living nearly two hundred years after Antiochus, referred to the setting up of the abomination in the Holy Place as a *future* event (Matthew 24:15; 2 Thessalonians 2:4; Revelation 13:15).

However, the deeds that Antiochus did and the deeds that the Antichrist will do are so very similar as to their nature, duration, and to the same target—Israel—that many scholars, including Fausset, Scoffield, and George Ladd, believe that Antiochus was definitely a type or forerunner of the Antichrist.

Not only is this blending of Antiochus with the Antichrist seen in Daniel 8 but also in Daniel 11. In Daniel 11:21–35 Antiochus is clearly in view while the Antichrist is seen in the verses that follow (36–45).

From what country will the Antichrist emerge? One must not be dogmatic here. If the little horn of Daniel 8:9 represents *only* Antiochus, then the Antichrist could come from any part of the vast Roman Empire or possibly outside of it, according to Daniel 7:20–26 where the Antichrist is clearly in view. Incidentally, the Roman Empire embraced parts of several of the Soviet Socialist Republics of today.

However, if the little horn of Daniel 8:9 represents an intimate blending of both Antiochus and the Antichrist as the verses that follow it suggest, *then the Antichrist can only come from one of the four divisions of Alexander's empire.* If commentators had only kept in mind this likely possibility, then they would not have brought the whole subject of prophecy into disrepute a few decades ago by loudly proclaiming that Hitler or Mussolini was the Antichrist. At no time was Germany or Italy a part of Alexander's empire.

The Bible does not specify which one of the four divisions of that empire will produce the Antichrist. However, since there is such an intimate blending of Antiochus with the Antichrist, one would be much more right than wrong in assuming that the Antichrist will arise as did Antiochus from the territory of the ancient Syrian Empire.

Because of this fact, one should note the nations today that occupy the territory of that ancient empire. Roughly they are Pakistan, Afghanistan, Iraq, Iran, Jordan, Syria, Lebanon, and parts of at least three Soviet Socialist Republics of the USSR (Armenian, Moldavian, and Turkmen SSR).

Which of these countries would be the most likely one to produce the Antichrist? It is hard to imagine any of the rigid Moslem nations giving up their religion to worship the Antichrist. Considering the utterly godless character of the Soviet ideologies, the Soviet Union would appear to be the most probable spawning ground to produce a godless Antichrist.

In Daniel's next vision his portrait of the Antichrist cannot be mistaken for any personage in history. Daniel 9:27 shows the tricky tyrant in action. Clearly one sees him make a seven-year treaty with Israel, break it after 3½ years, prohibit the Israelis from worshipping in their temple, and then "utterly defile the sanctuary of God" (v.27 LP). He exits with the wrath of God destroying him.

Israel make a seven-year treaty with her arch enemy—Russia? If she does and if the treaty is widely known, then one will have another in a long chain of clues which indicates that Russia will produce the Antichrist.

In tracking down an unknown criminal, detectives carefully question every witness and then give all the clues to an artist who then makes a portrait of the rascal. Every known detail is incorporated into the picture. This is then published in the papers and shown on television in the hope that someone will be able to recognize the criminal.

If any unprejudiced person would study only Daniel's portrait of the Antichrist, he should readily identify that tyrant when he appears on the world's stage.

One should keep the main features of Daniel's portrait in mind. With these he should keep seeking to identify the nation most likely to produce this future ruler. Here are the chief distinctives:

1 He may emerge from a country within the bounds of the ancient Grecian Empire (Daniel 8:9). Parts of at least three Soviet Socialist Republics seem to be included in that empire.

2 His ideology is different from preceeding nations (7:24).

3 He can be recognized by his blatant defiance of God and his persecution of God's followers (7:25).

4 He has "great shrewdness and intelligence" and "is skilled in intrigues" (8:23 LP with footnote).

5 He is characterized by his take-over of other nations (7:24).

6 He is nihilistic—destroys "all laws, morals and customs" (7:25). Russia originated nihilism in the 19th century.

7 The time of his appearance is dated: "the last days" or "that final event in history" (8:17,19; 12:4,9,13).

8 The length of his persecution of Israel is repeatedly given as 3½ years (7:25; 9:27; 12:7).

One must ever keep all of his ideas about the Antichrist fluid. His thinking must never petrify. He should know what other inspired prophets of the Bible say. In the next chapter one discovers other important identifications of this world figure as given by the Apostle John.

17

WILL ONE NATION RULE THE WORLD?

Revelation 13

Will one nation rule the world someday? Experts state that the society and culture of the past four hundred years is now senile and ready to die. An inkling of their views can be seen by noting the titles of books written by these noted scholars:

Gregg Singer, *The Collapse of Western Culture.*
Oswald Spengler, *The Decline of the West.*
Arnold J. Toynbee, *Civilization on Trial.*
James Burnham, *The Struggle for the World.*

Alfred Weber, *Farewell to European History*.

N. Berdyaev, *The End of our Time*.

Albert Einstein, *Ideas and Opinions*.

Frank Laubach, *Wake up or Blow up*.

Pitirim A. Sorokin, *The Crisis of Our Age*.

Pitirim A. Sorokin, *Man and Society in Calamity*.

(See *Guide*, Appendix 36 for sample of a few views.)

These experts give logical reasons for their conclusions. Nations are bankrupting themselves with huge military expenditures. Inflation and unrest among minority groups are reaching the explosive stage. Monetary crises plague the individual nations. Crime, drugs, violence, and arson fanned by communistic propaganda could readily get out of control. Last and most important the real danger of nuclear, bacteriological, and chemical extinction is imminent.

Most of these threats would be eliminated if one supranational power ruled all the nations.

However, most nations are much too nationalistic to surrender their own ways at a conference table. The spirit of "Give me liberty or give me death" is much too strong. A peaceful surrender of national sovereignties is most unlikely.

For a military take-over, only two nations are strong enough to head a world government—the United States and the Soviet Union.

The United States has never sought nor wanted the job of policing the world. It is still licking its sores from two world wars, plus the Korean and the Viet Nam wars. Indications are that the spirit of the 1970s may be isolationist.

In contrast, the Soviet Union has repeatedly announced her determination to "bury the United States" and to dominate the world. And if one looks at a world map, he will be surprised how much of the world the USSR controls completely or partially. Her only threat today to complete world control is the United States. (Later China may become a potent rival.)

Even the United States is reportedly honeycombed with Communists and pink sympathizers from the Pentagon down. In the 1960s organized radical groups repeatedly showed their power to disrupt public gatherings and terrorize universities with bombs, arson, and violence. Almost invariably the universities acceded to utterly absurd demands. If the United States cannot control the burning and devastation of her major cities in peace times, she could be completely stymied by sabotage in any war with Russia.

The radical groups are demoralizing America in ever increasing measure. They have cleverly popularized drug addiction, pornography, sexual promiscuity, nudity, abortion-on-demand, violence, and crime. With them only squares respect the flag, property rights, democracy, and the church. The sooner the whole Establishment and law and order are destroyed the better they would like it.

This is the pattern of the day, and the government and the church are impotent against this giant threat to society. If this trend continues, and there is no indication that it will not, then Russia can take the United States over without any war. As Khrushchev once said, "Like an overripe fruit, the United States will fall into the lap of the Soviets."

From all human projections, if a superpower will be ruling over the world in the foreseeable future, that nation will be Russia.

Toynbee, in *Civilization on Trial,* and Einstein, in *Ideas and Opinions,* are confident that one superpower will rule the world. Both fervently hope it will be the result of peaceful means but both are fearful that it may take a devastating, perhaps a nuclear, war.

Now consider what the Bible says about a world government and the tyrant who heads it. Will it be established by peaceful means or by war?

Revelation 6 predicts a frightful war, followed by a monstrous famine and deadly pestilence. The total death toll is an unthinkable 850 million people—"kill a fourth part of the earth" (Revelation 6:8 KJV).

After such a slaughter it is highly logical that the victor will control practically all the world.

The Bible does not name the winner but gives a strong clue about the ideology of that nation. After giving the total mortality figure, the next verse reveals a great company of people martyred "for the word of God and for the testimony which they held" (6:9 KJV). It certainly seems that the leader of this supranation is utterly godless and determined to wipe God's people off the earth.

Turning to Revelation 13, one discovers much about this great superpower and its blasphemous dictator. The Apostle John describes him:

> As I stood on the sandy beach, I saw a beast coming up out of the sea with ten horns . . . and seven heads. On his horns he had ten royal crowns . . . and blasphemous titles . . . on his heads. (13:1 AMPLIFIED)

Saw a beast coming out of the sea. Therion, a wild beast. *Beast* is the descriptive name used for the Antichrist in Revelation. *Sea* symbolizes "peoples and multitudes and nations and tongues" (17:15). The *Beast* can refer to either the Antichrist or his empire. A great emperor once said of himself, "I am the Empire." The empire is in view here since the "ten horns" represent ten kings or nations (Daniel 7:24; Revelation 17:12).

John was an independent observer, not a copyist. John adds many details not recorded by Daniel. Three times John adds that this Beast has seven heads (Revelation 12:3; 13:1; 17:3).

Seven heads and ten horns. This formula John also used in describing Satan (12:3). Such close similarity is understandable since it is Satan who puts his own trademark on the Antichrist and his empire (13:4).

Blasphemous titles on his heads. The identifying mark of this man and his empire is blatant godlessness. This should be most helpful since this designation could not apply as forcibly to any nation until the rise of Russia.

> And the beast that I saw resembled a leopard, his feet were those of a bear, and his mouth was like that of a lion. And to him the dragon gave his [own] might *and* power and his [own] throne and great dominion. (13:2 AMPLIFIED)

This empire of the future will have the militant potential of all empires of history (Daniel 7:1–6). It will have the cunning and speed of Alexander's leopard kingdom. One also sees the massive spread and manpower of the Medo-Persian bear. It will have the Babylonian's mouth of a lion to devour all foes. Thus equipped, this future empire and the Antichrist will seem to be invincible.

To him the dragon gave his own power (MOFFATT). Here is a very special endowment! Satan will give to the Antichrist what he offered to Jesus—all the kingdoms of this world. And today it is his to give (Luke 4:1–6; John 12:31; 14:30). Satan has ever been the leader of the Now generation and philosophy. Jesus refused Satan's offer of the mess of pottage because His eyes could see the day when "the kingdoms of this world are become the kingdoms of our Lord" (Revelation 11:15 KJV). He could discern the difference between the pleasure for the *now* and that for eternity.

> And I saw one of his heads as though it had been smitten unto death; and his death-stroke was healed: and the whole earth wondered after the beast.
> And they worshipped the dragon because he gave his authority unto the beast; and they worshipped the beast, saying, "Who is like unto the beast? and who is able to make war with him?" (13:3,4 ASV)

(The symbolism of the seven heads is explained in *Guide*, Appendix 41.)

The highly successful methods of a Satanically inspired Antichrist will cause the whole world to worship Satan and his Antichrist—which even today is common in many parts of the country.

Who is able to make war with him? Here and in the verses that follow is another Scriptural prediction of a world empire headed by an utterly godless ruler! He has so successfully squelched opposition that the rhetorical question is asked, "Who can make war with him?" All opposition is cowed.

The Antichrist now mouths the sentiments of the indwelling devil:

> The beast was allowed to mouth bombast and blasphemy, and was given the right to reign for forty-two months. He opened his mouth in blasphemy against God, reviling his name and his heavenly dwelling. (13:5,6 NEB)

Was allowed. . . . was given. . . . was permitted (v.7). Every activity of the Antichrist and Satan is under God's control. One must never forget this encouraging fact.

Was given the right to reign for forty-two months. (3½ years) At least five times one is reminded that the rule of the Antichrist is only 3½ years (Daniel 7:25; 9:27; 12:7; Revelation 12:14; 13:5). Twice God emphasizes that fact by raising his hand to heaven and swearing "that there shall be delay no longer" when the 3½ years are finished (Daniel 12:7; Revelation 10:5-7). That promise should encourage, when persecution hits as indicated in the next verses:

> . . . Moreover, it was permitted to make war upon the saints and to conquer them; the authority given to it extended over every tribe and people and language and nation. All the inhabitants of the earth will worship it—all whose names have not been written in the book of life which belongs to the Lamb slain from the foundation of the world. (13:7, PHILLIPS)

Make war upon the saints. Christians must ever remember that they are repeatedly warned of persecution during this Great Tribulation (6:9,10; 7:13,14; 12:17; 13:7,15; 20:4). One would do well to memorize what Jesus admonished about this same period:

> . . . For then comes the time when men will hand you over to persecution and kill you. And all nations will hate you because you bear my name. Then comes the time when many will lose their faith and will betray and hate one another. Yes, and many false prophets will arise, and will mislead many

people. Because of the spread of wickedness the love of most men will grow cold, though the man who holds out to the end will be saved. (Matthew 24:9–13 PHILLIPS)

If any man hath an ear, let him hear (Revelation 13:9 ASV). This admonition of Jesus occurs eight times in the gospels and eight times in Revelation. In every instance, except here, Jesus is specified as the speaker. He probably is the Speaker here, too.

Observe this important message from the Lord:

Whoever makes captives, he will be led into captivity; whoever kills with the sword, he must be killed by the sword. In this way the saints exercise their endurance and their faith. (13:10 BERKELEY)

J.B. Smith calls this the universal law of retribution: one is repaid with the same coin that he pays; what a man sows he shall reap; those who shed blood will die at the hand of another (Genesis 9:6); ". . . avenge not yourselves . . . I will repay, saith the Lord" (Romans 12:19 KJV).

The Lord does advise one to flee if that is possible (Matthew 24:16), but never to fight back. Imprisonment has redeeming features. Both Jesus and Paul considered this an opportunty to witness (Luke 21:13; Acts 16:30–34). Witnessing meant more than living to first-century Christians. So many paid with their lives for their witnessing that a witness (or, *martus*) became equivalent to *martyr* in the third century.

Note that the Antichrist has the help of a henchman:

Then I noticed another beast, that came up from the land. It had two horns like a lamb and it spoke like a dragon. It exercises the full authority of the first beast in its presence, and it makes the earth and those living in it to worship the first beast, whose mortal wound had been healed. (13:11,12 BERKELEY)

This beastly helper is wholly subservient to the Antichrist. He is also called the "false prophet" (16:13; 19:20; 20:10). His task is to make everybody worship the Antichrist.

Two horns like a lamb, and he spoke like a dragon. He is the devil in sheep's clothing. He wears the "cloth" but beneath will be found the hoofs and tail of Satan. He will present an impeccable ecclesiastical bearing but his mouthings will reek with brimstone.

And he doeth great signs, that he should even make fire to
come down out of heaven upon the earth in the sight of men.
And he deceiveth them that dwell on the earth by reason of
the signs which it was given him to do in the sight of the beast;
saying to them that dwell on the earth, that they should make
an image to the beast. . . . (13:13,14 ASV)

He deceiveth them that dwell on the earth. Deception is basic in the
work of Satan, the Antichrist, and the False Prophet (12:9; 18:23; 19:20;
20:3,8,10). Satan is incapable of performing a bona fide miracle. All his
signs are spurious. Yet these are highly successful with a gullible public.
Homo sapiens is much more *homo* than *sapiens!*

It was allowed to give breath to the image of the Beast, so that
it could speak, and could cause all who would not worship the
image to be put to death. (13:15 NEB)

Give breath (Greek *pneuma*) *to the image.* This is a more accurate
translation than that in the *King James Version of the Bible,* "give life
unto the image." The Greek word *pneuma* is found at least 383 times
in the New Testament and never translated "life" except here.

Most scholars do not believe that Satan has the power to give life to
any inanimate object. That is the prerogative of God alone. But this
ingenious robot can talk and gives the impression of being alive. It has
pneuma—breath, air or wind. Supply that to a robot with a mechanical
larynx, then it can talk, give orders and kill those who do not obey it.
Just one of Satan's deceptions, predicted by Jesus for these days (Matthew 24:24).

The False prophet goes to extremes to make people worship the
Antichrist:

Moreover it caused everyone, great and small, rich and poor,
slave and free, to be branded with a mark on his right hand
or forehead, and no one was allowed to buy or sell unless he
bore this beast's mark, either name or number. (Revelation
13:16,17 NEB)

Mark on his right hand or forehead. A tattoo mark would be readily
visible. No buying or selling without it. To be deprived of food, clothing, electricity, fuel, water, housing, medical, and dental care will put
terrific pressure on all to conform or face starvation.

Some Christians will receive the mark and rationalize, "The thing
that really counts is what I believe in my heart." Already one hears,

"Better Red than dead." That is the philosophy of the Now generation. But these should read the eternal results of receiving the mark of the Antichrist (14:9-11). They should also read the multitudinous rewards awaiting the overcomer (Revelation 2:7,11,17,26; 3:5,12,21; 7:14-17; 9:4; 12:14-16; 14:1-5, 13; 19:4-9; 20:4-6; 21 and 22).

Both in Daniel and Revelation, the Lord gives many identifying details to recognize the Antichrist. Finally, in this last verse, He gives a conclusive proof:

> Here is the key; and anyone who has intelligence may work out the number of the beast. The number represents a man's name, and the numerical value of his letters is six hundred and sixty-six. (13:18 NEB)

It was the custom of the ancients to give certain letters a numerical value. Adding up the numerical values of these letters in a person's name would give a figure—a secret identification number for that person. The Antichrist can be further identified, as the sum of numerical values in the letters of his name will be 666. J.B. Smith, in *A Revelation of Jesus Christ*, indicates that the Antichrist can be identified through numbers. (See *Guide*, appendix 37.)

Because the Lord has already given a multitude of ways to identify the Antichrist, one cannot help feeling gratitude to the God who also gives this ancient numerical device to clinch this future tyrant's identity.

Perhaps the Lord knows that when a person must make a decision involving the starvation and martyrdom of himself and his family, he should also have objective Scriptural proof from a mathematical standpoint. (A summary of the Antichrist is given in *Guide*, appendix 38.)

18

REJOICING OR REMORSE?

Revelation 14

This chapter offers a choice—rejoicing or remorse! One sees first the rejoicing of 144,000 Israelis because they heeded the Lord's admonition to flee Jerusalem when the Antichrist set up his abomination in the temple. As a result the Lord protected them from the greatest of all tribulations and cared for them for 3½ years (Matthew 24:16,21; Revelation 7:1–8; 9:4; 12:6,14).

After that experience, John now sees them in heaven playing their harps and singing. What a stupendous orchestra, what a thrilling choir of 144,000 voices! Introducing this heavenly performance is God with a voice like rolling thunder. John describes the scene.

> Then I looked and saw the Lamb standing on Mount Zion, and with Him 144,000, who had His name and His Father's name inscribed on their foreheads. And I heard a voice from heaven like the sound of many waters and like the peals of loud thunder. I then heard the music as of harpists playing on their harps.
> They were singing a new song before the throne and in the presence of the four living beings, and of the elders, and none was able to sing the song except the 144,000 that were purchased from the earth. (14:1–3 BERKELEY)

The Lamb standing on Mount Zion, with Him 144,000. As in Hebrews, *Mount Zion* refers to "Mount Zion . . . the heavenly Jerusalem and to an innumerable company of angels" (Hebrews 12:22 KJV). Since the 144,000 are "before the throne and in the presence of the four living beings and the twenty-four elders," the place must be heaven (Revelation 4 & 5). Furthermore, when the *earthly* Zion (Jerusalem) is in view in the New Testament, it is never preceeded by *Mount* (Matthew 21:5; John 12:15; Romans 9:33; 11:26; 1 Peter 2:6).

The 144,000 who had the Lamb's name and His Father's name inscribed on their foreheads. When these Israelis were first seen in Revelation 7:2, they only had "the seal of the living God." But here in Revelation 14 they also have the seal of the Lamb. Now they are Christians.

What events led to their conversion? One cannot be sure. Yet it was Jesus who explicitly predicted how the Israelis can escape the terrors of the Great Tribulation of the tomorrows. He stated that when they see the abominable image in the temple, that those in Judea should immediately flee (Matthew 24:15,16,21). In Revelation 12:6,14 one reads that the Israelis actually do flee to a divinely prepared shelter where God nurtures them during the 3½ years of the Great Tribulation. Both in the Matthew and the Revelation record, it seems that the Lord must be referring to the same group of Israelis, since their flight in both cases occurs just before the Great Tribulation.

What will be the reaction of those favored Israelis when they, with their loved ones, become safely established in the haven prepared by God? And especially when they hear of the horrible slaughter of the Israelis who would not heed the warning of Jesus!

When they further read that it was the same Jesus who predicted in the first century the destruction of the temple; the worldwide dispersion and persecution of the Jews; and later their regathering as a nation (1948); the recapture of Jerusalem (1967); the building of a future temple and the setting up of an abomination in the temple—what will be their attitude toward Jesus, the One protecting them? Will they have enough signs to accept Him as their Messiah?

It will certainly be strange if a revival and spiritual rebirth do not occur! In fact, the next verse states that they are "the first fruits unto God and to the Lamb" (Revelation 14:4 KJV). They are the first fruits of Israel. The later fruits of Israel will be garnered at the return of Christ when ". . . they shall look upon Him, whom they have pierced; they shall wail for Him as one wails for an only son . . ." (Zechariah 12:10 BERKELEY).

None was able to sing the song except the 144,000. Why? This group of Israelis have been miraculously delivered from Israel's greatest persecutions, worse even than Hitler's holocaust. Frightening to think of anything worse! Their gratitude for this physical deliverance and their joy at discovering their Messiah will know no bounds. No other group can quite sing the song of adoration that this group will proclaim.

On what basis were the 144,000 selected? Mention has been made of their obedience to Jesus' warning to flee. The next verses indicate they have other commendable spiritual qualifications.

> For they are spiritually undefiled, pure as virgins, following the Lamb wherever He goes. (Revelation 14:4 LNT)

> These were purchased from among men, to be the first fruits unto God and . . . the Lamb. And in their mouth was found no lie: they are without blemish. (14:4,5 ASV)

There is a closely parallel drama in Ezekiel 8 and 9. Apparently the Jewish exiles in ancient Babylon were complaining to Ezekiel about God's exiling them. To reveal why God had chastised them, God took Ezekiel, in the spirit, back to Jerusalem. There Jehovah showed Ezekiel the immoralities of the religious leaders of that day. In the holy temple behind locked doors, these leaders were participating in the vilest of sexual perversions while their lustful eyes reveled in the vile images portrayed on the walls.

Then Ezekiel saw six men each with "a slaughter weapon in his hand" (KJV). Before these men destroyed Jerusalem, one of them went ahead and put a protective seal "upon the foreheads of the men who bewail and bemoan all the detestable impieties that are being practiced here" (Ezekiel 9:4 MOFFATT).

Just as it was in Ezekiel's day so will it be at the beginning of the Great Tribulation. Those Israelis who will receive God's protective seal on their foreheads will be those who have separated themselves from the vile immoralities of their day.

Translators have difficulty expressing the thought of Revelation 14:4. In *Living Prophecies* Kenneth Taylor gives the symbolic view, "For they are spiritually undefiled, pure as virgins." Here is one of many literal translations, "They are those not contaminated with women, for they are celibates" (Berkeley). Discussion of the literal view is given in *Guide*, Appendix 39.

The fact that *all* of the 144,000 are seen in heaven indicates that the Rapture has taken place. Evidently, it has just occurred and just before the last proclamation of the gospel goes out to a wicked world. Since all the Christians are in heaven, God now resorts to angels to give His message. This is the first exhortation:

> And I saw another angel flying through the heavens, carrying the everlasting Good News to preach to those on earth—to every nation, tribe, language and people.
> "Fear God," he shouted, "and extol His greatness. For the time has come when He will sit as Judge. Worship Him who made the heaven and the earth, the sea and all its sources." (Revelation 14:6,7 LNT)

This appeal pulsates with the heartthrob of God Himself. It is effective preaching since the gospel is heard by every tribe and in every man's tongue. J.B. Smith believes that this is the fulfillment of the sign that Jesus gave of the time of the end, "And this gospel . . . shall be preached in all the world . . . then shall the end come" (Matthew 24:14 KJV).

Another angel shows the fallacy of depending on a certain false religion:

> Then another angel, a second, followed, and he cried, "Fallen, fallen is Babylon the great, she who has made all

126

nations drink the wine of God's wrath upon her fornication!
(Revelation 14:8 NEB, marginal reading)

Babylon is the mystery name for Rome and Romanism. She is the harlot of Revelation 17 who controls "peoples and multitudes and nations and tongues" (17:15 KJV). When the world hears that this great ecclesiastical religion who rode and directed the policies of nations— this vast church which made herself impregnable with vast ecumenical accretions—to be told that this system with its hundreds of millions of adherents has fallen—this announcement will surely jar many into reconsidering their alignments.

> Yet a third angel followed, crying out loud, "Whoever worships the beast and its image and receives its mark on his forehead or hand, he shall drink the wine of God's wrath, poured undiluted into the cup of his vengeance. He shall be tormented in sulphurous flames before the holy angels and before the Lamb. The smoke of their torment will rise forever and ever, and there will be no respite day or night for those who worship the beast and its image or receive the mark of its name." (14:9–11 NEB)

Today hellfire and brimstone preaching has gone out of the pulpits. But here God's messengers proclaim the whole truth. Seminary President Walvoord writes about the torment:

> Their torment is not a momentary one, for it is described in v.11 as continuing forever, literally "into the ages of ages," the strongest expression of eternity of which the Greek is capable.

J.B. Smith reminds the skeptical reader that anyone disposed to discredit the Biblical teaching on the eternal destiny of the wicked should be reminded that Jesus and His beloved disciple said more in regard to this doctrine than all the remaining contributors to the New Testament. Not only is a warning given to the wicked but an earnest exhortation fortifies the Christians in the final hours of the Tribulation:

> Let this encourage God's people to endure patiently every trial and persecution, for they are His saints who remain firm to the end in obedience to His commands and trust in Jesus. (14:12 LNT)

Jesus also exhorted His followers to persevere in the trying days of the Great Tribulation, ". . . he that shall endure unto the end, the same shall be saved!" (Matthew 24:13 KJV). Also see Revelation 13:10.

> Then I heard a voice from Heaven saying, "Write this! From henceforth happy are the dead who die in the Lord!" "Happy indeed," says the Spirit, "for they rest from their labors and their deeds go with them." (14:13 PHILLIPS)

Observe the One who makes this promise—God's Holy Spirit. What a contrast between the remorse of those who die with the mark of the Beast upon them and those who, though martyred, awake to an eternity of rejoicing.

Following this final gospel message, the wrath of God descends:

> Then I looked and saw a white cloud and One seated on the cloud, One like a Son of Man. On His head He wore a golden crown and in His hand was a sharp scythe. (14:14 BERKELEY)

Son of Man. This title is applied to Jesus eighty-four times in the Gospels, according to J.B. Smith. Returning to this earth on a cloud is a fulfillment of Jesus' prediction (Matthew 24:30). The crown of gold signifies His regal authority while the scythe symbolizes judgment and wrath.

> Another angel came out of the temple, who shouted with a mighty voice to the One seated on the cloud: "Thrust in your scythe and reap, for the harvest time has come, because the earth's harvest is overripe."
> So, the One seated on the cloud swung His scythe on the earth and the earth was harvested. (14:15,16 BERKELEY)

The earth's harvest is overripe. Overripe is better than ripe as in the King James Version. J. B. Smith states that the Greek word used here is usually translated *withered—withered* hand (Mark 3:1,3); *withered* branch (John 15:6); withered seedling (Luke 8:6). A withered product requires cutting and burning.

Son of Man . . . in His hand was a sharp scythe. Many Scriptures affirm that Jesus is the Executor of judgment (John 5:22; Psalm 2:12; Revelation 19:11–16).

Again, another angel came out from the heavenly temple, who likewise had a sharp scythe. Yet another angel came forth from the altar, who had authority over the fire, and he called with a mighty voice to the one with the sharp scythe, "Thrust in your sharp scythe and harvest the clusters of earth's vine, for its grapes are overripe."

So the angel swung out his scythe on the earth and stripped the earth's vine and threw it into the great winepress of God's indignation. (14:17–20 BERKELEY)

The grapes were trodden outside the city, and out of the winepress flowed blood for two hundred miles in a stream as high as the horses' bridles. (14:20 PHILLIPS)

Out of the winepress flowed blood for two hundred miles in a stream as high as the horses' bridles. This language may well be symbolic. I thought it must be figurative speech until I talked with a French soldier who was at the great battle of Liege in World War II. The Germans had to push through here in order to get to France. Wave after wave of Germans stormed over the dead bodies of their comrades only to be mowed down by French machine-gun fire. Thus failing, the Germans then sent their huge tanks crunching over the bodies of their dead and dying.

Sitting at our dining table out in Africa, the French soldier hesitated in his recital. Shaking his head and grimacing he continued, "After these monster tanks crushed the big pile of bodies, they left in their wake . . . a river of blood. The blood flowed as deep as your dining table."

Previously (9:16), John emphasized that the army from the Orient would number 200 million.

Is two hundred miles too long? If this army of 200 million extended two hundred miles, it would still have a concentration of one million soldiers per mile. Understandable how the blood could be as high as "the horses' bridles" in strategic areas!

To convey accurate concepts with about a dozen feeble words is most difficult. I doubt if John meant that the blood would have a uniform depth of about three feet for all of the two hundred miles.

However, one must be careful not to judge future wars with the little yardsticks of the past. Revelation 14:14–20 is describing the slaughter when God pours out His wrath on the wicked armies of the world bent on destroying His city and His chosen people. Here is not one army of

200 million but all the armies of *all nations* converging on Jerusalem (Zechariah 12:3; 14:2).

They have two objectives: (1) "They have said, Come, and let us cut them off from being a nation that the name of Israel may be no more in remembrance" (Psalm 83:4 KJV); (2) They have gathered "to take a spoil, and to take a prey . . ." (Ezekiel 38:12 KJV). The Middle East has great geographical importance and vast natural resources that both Russia and China are seeking.

These ungodly nations do succeed in devastating Israel (Zechariah 13:8,9). Then God in His fury enters the conflict (Ezekiel 38:18–22; 39:2–6; Zechariah 14:3–7). God uses the same method that He often used to defeat Israel's foes, "I will summon an utter panic against him . . . till every man in his host shall draw the sword against his fellow . . ." (Ezekiel 38:21 MOFFATT). Same expression is seen in Zechariah 14:13. Little wonder that almost 84 percent of some armies perish (Ezekiel 39:2).

God produces the panic by darkening sun, moon, and stars; by sending the greatest earthquake of all times; by causing deafening thunder, lightning, huge hailstones, and balls of fire (Matthew 24:29,30; Revelation 6:12–17; 11:15–19; 16:17–20; Isaiah 13:9–13; Ezekiel 38:19,20; 39:6; Joel 2:10; 3:15; Zechariah 14:4–6).

When these hundreds of millions of soldiers, equipped with ultramodern weapons of every kind, panic in the darkness and confusion, they will throw everything they possess upon one another. No need to quibble over how deep the blood flows. All one can say with certainty is that the Apostle John is describing a military and civilian slaughter defying description with any words, metaphors, or symbols.

19

GOD BATTLES THE ANTICHRIST

Revelation 15 and 16

The trumpets portrayed the devastation wrought by Satan and his Antichrist. The bowls of God's wrath depict His overwhelming punishment of these wicked destroyers of earth and its inhabitants.

Then I saw another sign in Heaven, vast and awe-inspiring: seven angels are holding the seven last plagues, and with these the wrath of God is brought to an end. (15:1 PHILLIPS) I saw what seemed a sea of glass shot with fire, and beside the sea of glass, holding the harps which God had given them, were those who had won the victory over the beast and its image and the number of its name. (15:2 NEB)

Sea of glass shot with fire. The fire is a portent of coming judgment on the allies of the Antichrist who had martyred many of these Christians. Their refusal to worship him had cost them torture and death. But now in heaven they are relishing the first fruits of their faithfulness. What a tremendous scene! Standing beside the colored sea with harps in their hands they sing:

They sang the song of Moses, the servant of God, and the song of the Lamb: "Great and marvelous are Thy works, Lord God the Omnipotent; just and true are Thy ways, O King of the nations. Who will not revere and glorify Thy name, O Lord? For Thou alone art holy. For all the nations shall come and worship before Thee, because Thy sentences of judgment have been made known." (15:3,4 BERKELEY)

Sang the song of Moses. These saints have much in common with the Israelites of old who sang their song after the deliverance at the Red Sea. Both groups conquered in spite of severe persecutions.

After this, as I looked, the sanctuary of the heavenly Tent of Testimony was thrown open, and out of it came the seven angels with the seven plagues. They were robed in fine linen, clean and shining, and had golden girdles round their breasts. (15:5,6 NEB)

Opening the heavenly sanctuary is a portent of impending judgment (11:19; 16:17). This time is no exception.

Then one of the four living creatures gave the seven angels seven golden bowls full of the wrath of God who lives for ever and ever; and the sanctuary was filled with smoke from the glory of God and his power, so that no one could enter it until the seven plagues of the seven angels were completed. (15:7,8 NEB)

Smoke from the glory of God and His power. Smoke suggests awe and reverence in dealing with the majesty and holiness of God (Exodus 19:18; Isaiah 6:4). It forbids any to enter or interfere with the execution of the wrath of God.

> Then from the sanctuary I heard a loud voice, and it said to the seven angels, 'Go and pour out the seven bowls of God's wrath on the earth.'
> So the first angel went and poured his bowl on the earth; and foul malignant sores appeared on those men that wore the mark of the beast and worshipped its image. (16:1,2 NEB)

Before the discovery of the atomic bomb, any literal interpretation was too fantastic. But today it makes the most sense. At Hiroshima and Nagasaki many of the survivors developed painful, slowly healing ulcers of the skin. Ulcers of the digestive tract caused dysentery and massive internal hemorrhages.

Sores appeared on those men that wore the mark of the beast. Only those who have his mark suffer! Keep that fact in mind, as one sees the same pattern in the bowls that follow.

> The second angel poured his bowl on the sea, and it turned to blood like the blood from a corpse; and every living thing in the sea died.
> The third angel poured his bowl on the rivers and springs, and they turned to blood. (16:3,4 NEB)

Like the blood from a corpse. This is dark, watery, and putrid. What a stench when every living thing in the sea, rivers, and springs die! What a scene with countless trillions of dead fish floating on the surface! Bloody repulsive water everywhere in the area affected! And no other water to drink!

Will this judgment of God affect the whole world or be confined to the countries allied with the Antichrist? Keep in mind that in ancient Egypt the persecutors of Israel were the ones primarily affected by the plagues and other misfortunes (Exodus 8:22; 9:6,26; 10:23; 12:13).

Furthermore, the verses that immediately follow indicate that only those godless nations who martyred God's people will need to drink this utterly repulsive water:

> . . . And I heard the angel of the waters say:
> "Just art thou in these thy judgments, thou who art and wast the holy one! For they have spilled the blood of saints and

prophets, and now thou hast given them blood to drink. They
have what they deserve."

And I heard the altar say,

"Yes O Lord, God Almighty, thy judgments are true and
right." (16:5–7 PHILLIPS)

The angel over the waters of seas, rivers, and springs attests to the
righteousness of God's judgments. He ought to know for he had seen
how the Antichrist, to an innocent nation, had turned a part of the
waters of the sea, the rivers, and the springs to blood when the second
and third trumpets blew (Revelation 8:8,9).

The altar also justifies God's act because these wicked men of the
Antichrist had "spilled the blood of saints and prophets." The altar
ought to know—under it were the souls of these martyrs (6:9–11).

There is significance in the fact that while the Antichrist performed
his evil deeds under the *second and third* trumpets, God punished
them in the *second and third* bowls of His wrath. Many, many Scriptures reveal that God often punishes in the same pattern or with the
same coin. Just as the Antichrist used the sun to afflict people in the
blowing of the *fourth* trumpet (8:12), God now uses the same sun to
punish the Antichrist in the fourth bowl of His wrath:

The fourth angel emptied his bowl over the sun, and the sun
was given power to scorch men in its fiery blaze. Then men
were terribly burned in the heat, and they blasphemed the
name of God who has control over these afflictions; but they
neither repented nor gave him glory. (Revelation 16:8,9 PHIL-
LIPS)

The sun was given power to scorch men. Professor Gorden J.F. Mac-
Donald, Associate Director of the Institute of Planetary Physics at the
University of California describes how man may soon produce such
burns. One of the layers of the stratosphere is the ozone layer about
nine to thirty miles above the earth. This ozone absorbs the greater
part of the lethal ultraviolet rays from the sun. Without this filtering
effect every living animal and plant would be killed.

Today scientists are experimenting with "burning holes" in this
ozone layer. Once they can do this efficiently they will have a deadly
weapon to either scorch men or kill them. If the hole is large, a whole
nation could be scorched!

It is most helpful to compare each bowl with the corresponding
trumpet. Geography is important in the study of the fifth trumpet and
bowl. Under the fifth trumpet flying agents went out from the abyss,

the symbolic name of the country of origin of the Antichrist (9:2–11; 11:7; 17:8). One cannot help wonder if only Israel suffers this torture —because the only group, mentioned as being protected from it, is the 144,000 Israeli.

Be that as it may, Israel is certainly one nation that is hit by the flying agents of torture which emerge from the country of the Antichrist. That was the *fifth* trumpet. Now observe under the *fifth* bowl how God punishes the Antichrist for his attack on Israel:

> The fifth angel poured his bowl on the throne of the beast; and his kingdom was plunged in darkness. Men gnawed their tongues in agony, but they only cursed the God of heaven for their pains and sores, and would not repent of what they had done. (16:10,11 NEB)

His kingdom was plunged in darkness. The professor of planetary physics writes in *Unless Peace Comes:*

> . . . In principle it would be feasible to introduce material into the upper atmosphere that would absorb either incoming light (thereby cooling the surface) or outgoing heat (thereby warming the surface).

Men gnawed their tongues in agony . . . cursed God . . . and would not repent. Here is the stance of a nation long trained and deeply entrenched in hostility toward God. Rather than simply repent and be free of terrible agony, they gnawed their own tongues—the reasoning of an angry infant who pounds his head on the floor. This is the height of perversity and rebellion against God!

On the throne of the Beast and his kingdom. The first six bowls of God's wrath seem to be primarily directed against the Antichrist and his subjects while, as one will later see, the *seventh* or final bowl affects wicked people everywhere. (See chart in Chapter 8, Chronology of The Revelation.) In the first bowl painful ulcers came upon those who had the mark of the Beast. In the second and third bowls, those who had bloody putrid water to drink were thus punished because these wicked men "had spilled the blood of the saints and prophets." The fourth bowl seems to have been poured out on the same godless group because they would not repent but blatantly blasphemed God. In the fifth bowl the target is clearly stated—the throne of the Beast and his kingdom. Likewise, one will shortly see that the sixth bowl is also directed against the Antichrist and the armies of his allies.

> The sixth angel poured his bowl on the great river Euphra-
> tes; and its water was dried up, to prepare the way for the
> kings from the east. (16:12 NEB)

The kings from the east, poised on the Euphrates River! The Euphrates River has one's attention in this *sixth* bowl just as it had in the *sixth*
trumpet. Under that sixth trumpet John was emphatically told that the
great army from the east numbered 200 million (9:16). Because this
army is so stupendous, God dries up the river to expedite the crossing.

Why can this sixth bowl qualify to be a bowl of God's wrath? As
previously noted, the first six bowls of God's wrath are all directed
against the Antichrist and his allies firmly rooted in hostility toward
God. God helps this army because He knows they will tangle with the
Antichrist and his allies and destroy them. In fact, this army from the
east will "kill a third of mankind" (9:15 LNT). Helping this army from
the east is a blow to the Antichrist. Hence, this bowl in its purpose
harmonizes with the others.

Why is the Euphrates River given the center of the stage in the sixth
trumpet and the sixth bowl? One cannot be positive in answering.
However, in the discussion of the sixth trumpet, evidence was presented that the Euphrates River seems to be the future eastern boundary of Israel.

From the day that God promised Abraham and his descendants all
the land from the river of Egypt to the Euphrates River (Genesis
15:18), this river has been kept fresh in Hebrew thought
(Deuteronomy 1:7; 11:24; Joshua 1:4; 2 Samuel 8:3; 2 Kings 24:7; 1
Chronicles 5:9; 18:3; Jeremiah 13:4–7; 46:2–10; 51:63). One cannot
read these references along with Revelation 9:14 and 16:12 without
being thrilled at this unity attesting to the inspiration of the Word.

Not only has the Euphrates River been engraved on Jewish thinking
but today the Euphrates River is chiseled on the stones of their parlia-
ment in Jerusalem. From Elizabeth Elliot's article in April, 1969,
Christian Herald listen to an Arab, an ex-mayor of the old city of
Jersualem, complain:

> On their parliament building, the Knesset, there is carved
> a statement that Israel shall extend from the Nile to the Eu-
> phrates. They will not forget this. We know that they will
> continue to expand.

God never promised to the Nile River but to the "river of Egypt,"
just below the Gaza strip. In 1967 Israel captured this river and territory to the west. And in this war Israel captured the Golan Heights and

Quentra, the strategic city for invading Syria. If Syria continues to harass Israel, Israel will probably extend her eastern border to the Euphrates River. If she does, then the meaning of the *Euphrates River* will have enhanced significance.

Satan, too, is a very clever planner in military strategy as the next verses indicate:

> Then I saw coming from the mouth of the dragon, the mouth of the beast, and the mouth of the false prophet, three foul spirits like frogs. (16:13 NEB)
> These miracle-working demons conferred with all the rulers of the world to gather them for battle against the Lord on that great coming Judgment Day of God Almighty.
> And they gathered all the armies of the world near a place called, in Hebrew, Armageddon—the Mountain of Megiddo. (16:14; 16 LNT)

The devil, the Antichrist, and the False Prophet—this infernal trinity unite to gather all nations to battle *against* God Almighty.

From these three go out invisible *miracle-working demons* to indwell and convince the rulers of the nations that they should send their armies to the Middle East. These demons do not tell them that they will be fighting God. That would be too fantastic! Perhaps, they stress the importance of the Middle East for world domination. That would be ideal bait to entice Russia and China.

Satan does succeed in getting them there as many Scriptures attest (Psalm 2:1–5; Zechariah 12:3,9; 14:2; Revelation 19:19).

Satan knows prophecy. He and his demons know that the *short time* of their freedom is over (Revelation 12:12). The time to bind him is now at hand (20:1,2).

He remembers the frightful war he did wage with God and lost (Revelation 12:7–9). But now impressed by all the vast armies of the world, with their huge stockpiles of nuclear bombs, their countless millions of tons of poison gases, their biological and geophysical weapons, a desperate but deluded Satan is determined to win.

John describes the forces of God and of Satan poised for action:

> Then I saw heaven wide open, and there before me was a white horse; and its rider's name was Faithful and True. . . . the armies of heaven followed Him on white horses. . . . Then I saw the beast and the kings of the earth and their armies mustered to do battle with the Rider and his army. (19:11,-14,19 NEB)

Referring to this very hour when these armies are poised for battle, a loving Father gives His last exhortation to Christians.

> 'That is the day when I come like a thief! Happy is the man who stays awake and keeps on his clothes, so that he will not have to go naked and ashamed for all to see!' (Revelation 16:15 NEB)

The day when I come like a thief! (refer to 1 Thessalonians 5:2). This is the time when the *last trump* shall sound, the time of the Rapture (1 Corinthians 15:52; Revelation 10:7 16:17). It is the time *just before* that terrible wrath of God is poured out on the world. It is the time when the seventh angel is *at the point of blowing* (Revelation 10:7 BERKELEY). The Lord at this juncture snatches His Bride before this last bowl is poured out:

> Then the seventh angel poured his bowl on the air; and out of the sanctuary came a loud voice from the throne, which said, 'It is over!' And there followed flashes of lightning and peals of thunder, and a violent earthquake, like none before it in history, so violent it was. The great city was split in three; the cities of the world fell in ruin; and God did not forget Babylon the great, but made her drink the cup which was filled with the fierce wine of his vengeance. Every island vanished; there was not a mountain to be seen. Huge hailstones, weighting perhaps a hundred weight, fell on men from the sky; and they cursed God for the plague of hail, because that plague was so severe. (16:17–21 NEB)

What about these vast armies that Satan will gather? What will be their reaction when lightning, thunder, and earthquakes unequaled in history occur? when every mountain is leveled? when the sun is blackened and the moon becomes red as blood? and the skies become full of shooting stars? when huge hailstones crash on them?

Speaking of this day and these armies, the Bible gives the answer.

> And on that day a terrible panic from the Eternal shall fall on them, every man seizing his neighbor and raising his hand against his neighbour. . . . (Zechariah 14:13 MOFFATT)

> I will summon an utter panic against him . . . till every man in his host shall draw the sword against his fellow. (Ezekiel 38:21 MOFFATT)

Each army thinks its allies have turned on them. Every soldier becomes a maniac. They throw at each other everything—nuclear bombs, poison gases, and as yet undiscovered horrors!

None of these calamities will hit the born-from-above Christian. The contents of all the bowls fall on those who stubbornly refuse to align themselves with Jesus Christ. And before the last, the most terrible, the worldwide bowl is poured out, the Lord will gather His own, living and dead, to be with Him eternally.

20

COMMUNISM VERSUS CATHOLICISM

One cannot fully appreciate Revelation 17 until he understands in some small depth the outstanding historical events since 1918. It is not enough to know *what* happened. One must discern *why* it happened!

During this time two colossal ideologies have been in opposition to one another—Catholicism and Communism. These two groups comprise over half of the world's population, but their struggle affects all the rest. History describes the events of World War II and the Vietnam War, but usually ignores the important roles of these two universal factions.

There will be no consideration of the religious aspects of the Roman church here—only its purely political activities.

With the rise of Communism and its dedication to destroy everything that Christendom stands for, it is understandable why Catholicism pulled out its sword to destroy it. Did not Peter pull out his sword to defend his Lord (Matthew 26:51–53; John 18:10,11)? Italy was one of the first battlegrounds. Mussolini organized the Fascists for aggressive nationalism and violently opposed Communism. The Vatican supported him.

Spain became a republic in 1931, disestablished the Roman church, and secularized education, but five years later a junta headed by General Franco unleashed civil war to overthrow the republic. He had the blessing of the Vatican, Mussolini, and Hitler. Franco was opposed by Russia.

The bloody civil war that followed took the lives of one million

Spaniards. A truly gory deluge to make Franco the dictator of Spain! Catholicism again became the state religion.

The Catholic church has exercised strong formative influence in Spain and Portugal where Franco and Salazar had long reigns as dictators. Of course, in these countries freedom of religion had been restricted, but no worse than in those countries dominated by Communism.

Not alone did the strife between Catholicism and Communism disrupt governments in Italy and Spain, but it shook or shattered many nations in Europe, Asia, and South America.

In fact, the clash of these two ideologies contributed to the explosive ingredient of World War II—Hitler the Fuehrer!

Germany was a democracy, but Hitler sought complete power. To this end Chancellor von Papen, a Catholic, asked President Hindenberg to ask Hitler to form a government. Hindenburg did, then Von Papen resigned, and soon Hitler was chancellor.

Hitler, assured of the firm support of Catholics, then sought another election to confirm his status. In March, 1933, Hitler received a whopping 17 million votes.

But to become an iron-fisted dictator in Germany, Hitler needed a two-thirds vote in the Reichstag. Some Catholic members supported Hitler and thus he became the Fuehrer of Germany!

Thus Cardinal Pacelli, the future Pope Pius XII, contributed to Hitler's attainment of the highest position possible in powerful Germany. It is indeed regrettable that the Vatican, in its worthy desire to wipe out godless Communism, assisted two powerful monsters—Mussolini and Hitler.

When the Catholic party was disbanded, Hitler gave the nod for the signing of a concordat with the church. This was signed in the Vatican with elaborate ceremonies by von Papen for Hitler and by Cardinal Pacelli for the Vatican on July 20, 1933.

Why did the Vatican accept Hitler? They saw in Hitler their only hope of destroying Communism, Christianity's greatest threat. Second, they also hoped that Hitler's persecution of German Catholics would cease.

Hitler benefited greatly from this concordat. Obedient to Clause 30 of that document, all Catholics prayed for Hitler every Sunday and every holy day. In line with Article 16, all bishops expressed loyalty to the Nazi regime.

Not only in Germany but in the neighboring countries, the Vatican helped Hitler as this record by Avro Manhattan in *Vatican Imperialism in the Twentieth Century* indicates:

In 1934 Hitler attempts to incorporate Austria and murders pocket-dictator Dolfuss. Austrian Catholics and the Vatican begin secret negotiations with the Fuehrer. In 1935 he gets the Saar, with the support of the Catholics. . . .

In 1936 Hitler occupies the Rhineland, again with the support of the Catholics. . . .

In 1937 Hitler disrupts Austria, with the help of Catholic Seyss-Inquart, Catholic Von Papen and Cardinal Innitzer.

In 1938 Hitler annexes Austria. Cardinal Innitzer welcomes Hitler in Vienna as a man of divine Providence. Hitler turns to Czechoslovakia. Again disrupters from within are Catholics. . . .

In 1939 Hitler occupies Czechoslovakia.

Rewarded for his dedicated leadership Cardinal Pacelli is elected Pope Pius XII.

One needs to remember that Pope Pius XII, while Cardinal Pacelli, was the cosigner of the concordat. Then one can understand why Pope Pius XII refrained from protest while Hitler slaughtered 6 million Jewish men, women, and innocent children. (See *Guide*, Appendix 40 for additional background.)

Communism also played a major role in the causation of World War II. When Hitler looked appraisingly at Poland in 1939, England and France made threatening gestures toward Germany, because of their treaty with Poland. Hitler hesitated because he also feared that his bitter enemy Russia might use the occasion to invade Germany.

Then the world got a big surprise! Hitler, after making friendly overtures to Russia, signed a nonaggression pact with Stalin. This pact between the bitterest of enemies amazed the world. It was a marriage between Nazism, the extreme right, and Communism, the extreme left!

In the United States, Communist Whitaker Chambers was dumbfounded until General W.G. Krivitsky explained "that this pact demonstrated Stalin's genius as a strategist." He said Stalin wanted to turn Hitler loose on Europe. After the European nations fought themselves to exhaustion, then Russia could readily take over Europe.

Hitler and Stalin signed the pact August 23, 1939. Just eight days later the German panzer divisions invaded Poland!

England and France then declared war on Germany and earth's greatest deluge of blood flooded Europe. Stalin must have chuckled at the success of his strategy which later did give him control in large parts of Europe.

Within months Hitler occupied Poland, Belgium, and France. The

British army barely managed to escape across the channel at Dunkirk.

On June 22, 1941, Hitler, elated by his successes, attacked the Soviet Union. Catholics approved the assault on their enemy—godless Communism, dedicated to wipe out Christianity!

As a result of unbelievable giveaways to Russia at the Yalta Conference, and the collapse of Germany, Russia gradually controlled or cowed much of Europe. Stalin's strategy and gun-barrel diplomacy worked miracles.

Not only did Russia get direct control of some European countries but the virus of Communism attacked the vital organs of most of the remaining countries. In fact, Italy, bastion of Catholicism, soon had one of the largest Communist parties in Europe.

The Roman hierarchy realized that they were no match for Communism in any direct confrontation. The Catholic party was rebuilt, but it was given a new name, Christian Democrat party. This new facade was more in harmony with the democratic architecture of the period.

Catholic influence was felt in a large part of Europe: Belgium, Holland, Austria, Switzerland, France, West Germany, and Italy, not to mention Spain and Portugal as well. Many premiers were zealous Catholics, such as De Gasperi in Italy and Adenauer in Germany.

In Hungary, Cardinal Mindszenty was accused of attempting to restore the monarchy of the House of Hapsburgs.

The Communists promptly accepted Cardinal Mindszenty's challenge for control of Hungary. Pathetically, the Hungarians were caught in the cross fire between the Catholics and the Communists. Tens of thousands of poor Hungarians perished. That Khrushchev was wholly lacking in any humane feeling was seen in his extreme treachery and cruelty. A summary of this story should be read by those naïve Americans who trust any treaty with the Soviet Union.

However, even before Pope Pius XII died in 1958, far-sighted personages in the Vatican saw the futility of direct confrontation with the more powerful Communists. The new pope, John XXIII, ushered in a new era and a new strategy. The goal was not changed, only the method. His policy was one of outward friendliness with the Communists.

And he was remarkably successful! Imagine the editor of Russia's official newspaper, *Izvestia*, going to Rome to visit Pope John! When Pope John gathered in world journalists to announce his new program, there sat Khrushchev's son-in-law. Although Queen Elizabeth created a great stir, she, too, went to pay her respects to the pope.

One should remember that the Catholic church assumed this conciliatory policy only in some countries. Nothing was changed in Spain,

Portugal, and in other nations where the church exerted strong influence.

Take Viet Nam as an example. To better understand the undercurrents of the Viet Nam War, take a look at the background of its former dictator, Diem. In his youth he wanted to be a priest. During the early French crisis, while in exile in the United States and Belgium, he always wanted to stay in Catholic monasteries and lead the austere life.

He was picked as Viet Nam's leader with the hope that such a rigid Catholic would never compromise with Communism. They could not have picked a better man for that issue!

But it was difficult to foresee another factor, Buddhism. In June, 1963, a Buddhist monk sat down cross-legged in a busy Saigon street. To his gasoline-soaked clothes, he calmly lit a match. His was a flaming protest to the persecution of the Buddhists. Previously he had written a note to Diem, "Enforce a policy of religious equality."

The burning of the monk was the culmination of a virulent campaign against the Buddhists by Dictator Diem and his two brothers. One brother was Nhu, the head of Viet Nam's secret police; the other was the Archbishop of Hue.

This determined threesome, controlling the government of Viet Nam, had for years been increasing a policy of discrimination and persecution against the Buddhists.

In a celebration to honor the Archbishop of Hue, the flag of the Vatican was flown without any protest from the Buddhists. But three days later, at the 2507th birthday of Buddha, the authorities prohibited the Buddhists from flying their religious flag. That discrimination was in a country where 80 percent of the people are practicing Buddhists!

When the Buddhists staged a peaceful demonstration against the edict, troops fired on the demonstrators and killed nine Buddhists. Then protest marches occurred all over South Viet Nam. Many casualties resulted.

In the army, bitter feuding broke out. The war effort became stalemated. Many Buddhists became Communists and agents for North Viet Nam. As a result, much of the military activity supported by American soldiers and money was nullified.

President John F. Kennedy was then in the White House. He repeatedly urged Diem to cool his persecution. He even suspended some of the huge subsidies such as those that financed the Catholic head of the secret police, Nhu.

No success! Nhu actually increased his persecution. Many were killed or tortured. Others saturated themselves with gasoline to become burning protests. Mrs. Nhu publicly scoffed at those monks who used "imported gasoline to barbecue themselves."

Naturally the whole war effort lagged and the general public became uncooperative—even hostile. The Communists made converts by the thousands. The army was ready to revolt.

President Diem and Nhu fled and hid in a small Catholic church. Buddhists found and killed them.

Any reference to the religious or theological aspects of the Roman church have been avoided here. The only purpose is to show that the Roman church is still a very active and powerful political organization.

Pathetically, many Buddhists and over 46 thousand American soldiers have already been killed in the cross fire between these two hostile ideologies. But this number is only a drop in the bucket compared to the many millions who perished in Spain, Hungary, and other countries, and in World War II when these two mighty forces played opposing but significant roles.

What will be the final outcome of this conflict between these two giants? Human speculations vary widely and are wholly unreliable. Yet these answers concern everybody. Fortunately Revelation 17 gives the Lord's answer and discernment for other questions of our perplexing times.

21

THE WOMAN RIDES THE "BEAST!"

Revelation 17:1–6

One of the seven angels who had the seven bowls then came
. . . to me, saying, Come with me! I will show you the doom
. . . of the great harlot [idolatress] who is seated on many
waters,
    [She] with whom the rulers of the earth have joined in
prostitution . . . and with the wine of whose immorality . . .
the inhabitants of the earth have become intoxicated. (Revelation 17:1,2 AMPLIFIED)

Who is this bizarre woman? The context indicates that a symbolic harlot is in view. Symbolic harlotry is frequently mentioned in the Bible. For instance, when Israel (the wife) forsook the love of Jehovah (her husband), she was repeatedly called a harlot (Leviticus 20:5,6;

Jeremiah 2:20; 3:1–8; Ezekiel 16:36; 23:7,30,37,43–49; Hosea 4:10–18).

In the New Testament, Christ and His church are symbolized as bridegroom and bride (John 3:29; Romans 7:4; 2 Corinthians 11:1–3; Ephesians 5:25–32; Revelation 19:7–9). It would certainly appear that the harlot that John saw was a church that forsook her Lord to seek one suited to her carnal desires.

The great harlot . . . with whom the rulers of the earth have joined. . . . Here is a church that ignored her religious priorities because of the enticements of worldwide political power over "the rulers . . . and the inhabitants of the earth." She was carried away by the lure of prestige and power.

Note that John the Apostle is not describing the *religious* aspect or the members of any church. But here and throughout this chapter John puts God's spotlight on the *hierarchy* of a certain church that is intently engaged in *political activities.* It is not the religious life but the political ambitions that are considered.

The great harlot who is seated on many waters. The symbolism of "many waters" is explained in verse 15, "The waters that you observed, where the harlot is seated are races and multitudes and nations and dialects." Impressive indeed is the far-reaching success of this church. Before one falls into that holier-than-thou trap to condemn any single church, one must recall that many churches have courted rulers for political gains. These churches are either not smart enough to be successful in the political game or they remembered that Jesus said, "My kingdom is not of this world" (John 18:36). The Bride of Christ, any part of it, will fail in her fidelity to her Lord, if she goes very far in her flirtations for political favors. There is an important lesson in this chapter for every church.

Who is this woman, this church? John states that she is a *city.* And he clearly identifies the city:

> And the woman that you saw is herself the great city which dominates *and* controls the rulers *and* the leaders of the earth. (Revelation 17:18 AMPLIFIED)

The only city that was controlling the world in John's day was Rome. One does not need further evidence, but verse 9 confirms this identification by referring to this city as having seven hills. In literary allusions Rome has often been described as "the city of seven hills" and was thus depicted on Roman coins.

Victorinus, the first commentator on Revelation, writing on verse 9's reference to the seven hills states, "That is the city of Rome." Also confirming that the city was Rome were church fathers such as Tertullian (160–230); Jerome (340–420); and Augustine (354–430).

Although the headquarters of this "woman" will be centered in Rome, one should not think of it as the Roman church of today. Human projections indicate that it will include millions of today's Protestants, Greek Orthodox, and even non-Christian groups. This future church will be an *ecumenical* organization, politically oriented. Considering the volcanic eruptions that are currently going on within the present Roman church and centering around such issues as divorce, abortion, and marriage of priests, it would be futile to speculate on the details of the structure of this church.

But this chapter does give some surprising details about the methods that this "new" church may use to gain control over the rulers and inhabitants of the world:

> And [the angel] bore me away . . . in the Spirit into a desert
> . . . , and I saw a woman seated on a scarlet beast that was all
> covered with blasphemous . . . names, and he had seven heads
> and ten horns. (Revelation 17:3 AMPLIFIED)

And the angel bore me away into a desert. A symbolic desert devoid of God and any reference to Him! Observe that John is now whisked away from the city where this church is based to the place where this red "beast" is located. A change in geography! This scarlet beast with the seven heads and the ten horns is the same godless international organization previously studied in detail. There evidence was submitted to indicate that this red confederacy of nations could be the United Nations or some future successor.

All covered with blasphemous names. That detail certainly fits the United Nations, so meticulously careful that prayer and God be strictly omitted from all its deliberations. The color of this "scarlet beast" is even relevant since Red Russia controls the largest voting bloc in the UN.

I saw a woman seated on a scarlet beast. This woman that John equated with Rome is now seen sitting on this international red beast. The Bible does not state when or how she mounted this godless organization.

On October 4, 1965, Pope Paul VI made an official visit to the United Nations. A CBS commentator reported, "Two unique and universal organizations came together today." Others said it was the beginning of a new era, a new epoch, a new age!

Indeed it was all of these, since it was a complete reversal of the bitter battles that the Vatican had waged with Red Communism from the latter's birth. Walter Cronkite stated that it looked like "the beginning of a crusade to help direct the nations to peace." A papal crusade to direct the nations!

One part of the Pope's speech to the United Nations showed superb horsemanship. He knew just what to say to tame and control this red beast:

> He who addresses you has not temporal power, nor any ambition to compete with you. In fact, we have nothing to ask for, no question to raise; we have at most a desire . . . of serving you in so far as we can, with disinterest, with humility and love. (*Christianity Today*, October 22, 1965)

While at the United Nations, Pope Paul tried to direct this obstreperous creature into two rocky pathways, where it had thrown all previous riders. He gave a strong pull on the right rein to keep the UN from going down the thorny path of birth control. Then a tug on the left rein as he spurred the beast to admit Communist China—a perennial reject.

And since that day the Pope has continued to tug on the reins. However, after five years of maneuvering, the UN has not taken any of the major roads that the Pontiff desired. That is understandable since Communism and Catholicism have ideologies entirely opposed to each other.

The UN will never really submit to the bit and bridle of any church. And it would seem that, as in the past so in the future, this godless beast will win because the Antichrist is endowed with all the authority and power of Satan himself (Revelation 13:4). Note how the Bible describes the final struggle between these international giants:

> And the ten horns that you saw, they and the beast will [be the very ones to] hate the harlot [the idolatrous woman]; they will make her desolate . . . and they will strip her, and eat up her flesh and utterly consume her with fire. (Revelation 17:16 AMPLIFIED)

Scripture identifies this woman more specifically:

> The woman herself was dressed in purple and scarlet, glittering with gold, jewels and pearls. (Revelation 17:4 PHILLIPS)

(See explanatory *Guide*, Appendix 41.)
John further describes this woman:

146

And on her forehead there was inscribed a name of mystery
—with a secret symbolic meaning: Babylon the great, the
mother of . . . idolatresses and of the filth *and* atrocities *and*
abominations of the earth. (Revelation 17:5 AMPLIFIED)

A name with a secret symbolic meaning. The apostle did not dare
to give the real name of Rome and then proceed to say uncomplimen-
tary things about it. That course would have brought the murderous
wrath of ancient Rome on all Christians. As previously noted he identified it indirectly. Now he gives it "a name with a secret symbolic
meaning"—Babylon.

How did that name identify the city as Rome? "Babylon" was chiseled deeply into the minds of all Jewry. Mere mention of it immediately brought to mind the Babylonish destruction of their beloved
Jerusalem; the sacking and destruction of God's temple; their harsh
exile to Babylon; and the unforgettable crack and bite of the whips of
the slave drivers. Through the centuries the name Babylon became
synonymous with a cruel merciless oppressor. In John's day to the Jew
that name meant only one city—Rome.

Is it too much to expect that some good Christian souls, for the first
time in their lives, may be awakened to what exists in their church and
will proceed to speak out against the existing evils within their church?
Can any Christian remain silent on evils that are worldwide? Here is
God's answer:

When I say unto the wicked, Thou shalt surely die; and thou
givest him not warning, nor speakest to warn the wicked from
his wicked way, to save his life; the same wicked man shall die
in his iniquity; *but his blood will I require at thine hand.*
(Ezekiel 3:18 KJV. Italics are mine.)

If warned some might find their voices to speak out against this last
evil that the Lord underlines:

Then I noticed that the woman was drunk with the blood of
the saints and of the martyrs for Jesus. As I watched her, I was
filled with utter amazement. (Revelation 17:6 PHILLIPS)

A glance will fill any honest reader with "utter amazement." Space
and fear of offending will not permit one to give even the briefest
summary of awful massacres over many centuries. One cringes from
any details about the slaughters, the tortures, and the burning alive of

147

millions of martyred Christians for such crimes as translating, printing, or even possessing any portion of the Bible. The records of these repugnant mass killings stain many a history book.

In conclusion, one should remember that the church which is predicted for the last days, although controlled by Rome, will *not* be the Catholic Church as one knows it today. Because it will include a large segment of Protestantism, its iron impact will be felt in every capital and hamlet of the world. It will ride and tug on the reins of the very powerful world government existing at that time. Although fantastically rich, and identifiable by the colors purple and scarlet, one must keep in mind that this apostate church will be an ecumenical church. It will embrace not only those *apostate* elements in the Roman and Greek Orthodox churches, but also countless millions from Protestantism, Judaism and humanism.

22

THE RED BEAST

Revelation 17:7–18:24

When Billy Graham was in Russia, he asked the meaning of the star on their red flag. *Decision Magazine* (April, 1970) reported that the guide promptly gave this reply:

> The five points stand for the five continents of the world. The red represents the blood that will have to be shed to bring the revolution to the world.

Twice the Apostle John specifies that the future ruler who will cause rivers of blood to flow throughout the world is red (Revelation 12:3; 17:3). This ruler, symbolized as a *beast*, has outstanding designations —seven heads and ten horns.

John strips all the disguises from this red ruler to reveal that he is actually "... that serpent of old that led the whole world astray, whose name is Satan, or the Devil ..." (12:9 NEB).

In this same chapter one discovers that the basic drive of this Satanic beast is the destruction of Israel and her Messiah. This fact is the key to understanding the beast's seven heads. Why is Satan dedicated to destroy Israel and her Messiah? He knows that Israel's Messiah is destined to destroy him and his demons (Genesis 3:15).

Three times John emphasizes that this beast has seven heads (12:3; 13:1; 17:3). John states that the seven heads have two symbolic meanings. The first meaning was taken up in the previous chapter. Now consider the second interpretation given by John:

> Here is the clue for those who can interpret it . . . They [the seven heads] represent also seven kings, of whom five have already fallen, one is now reigning, and the other is yet to come; and when he comes he is only to last for a little while. (17:9,10 NEB)

For those who can interpret it. John knew that there would be a great deal of difficulty interpreting this symbol. That is evident by the great variety of interpretations extant today. (See *Guide*, Appendix 42 for a summary of these.)

Here I shall give what seems to be the most logical interpretation of these seven kings.

One is now reigning. Nearly all interpreters agree that the reigning head in John's day was Emperor Domitian of the Roman Empire. In a totalitarian system the will of the emperor is really the will of the empire. One might say an emperor personifies his empire.

Five have fallen. Before John's day five world empires existed. In each of these five empires one can discover a specific king who almost exterminated Israel. Keep in mind that in Revelation 12 one discovered that the basic drive of the beast himself is the destruction of Israel and her Messiah.

1. Egypt was the first great power through which Satan tried to destroy the emerging nation of Israel and thus prevent the birth of the One destined to crush him. The Satanically controlled Pharoah of Moses' day ordered that every baby boy of the Israelites should be killed at birth. This edict and the harsh slavery of Egypt would soon have wiped Israel from the earth. But God intervened and miraculously brought the children of Israel out of Egypt.

2. Assyria under the leadership of Sargon carried ten of the twelve tribes into captivity and oblivion (2 Kings 17:5,6). Assyria tried to destroy the other two tribes without permission from God and suffered divine wrath (2 Kings 19:35,36; Isaiah 37:33–37).

3. Babylon and its great king Nebuchadnezzar became the next tool of Satan. Because of the stubborn refusal of Judah to repent of her unmentionable sins, God permitted Nebuchadnezzar to carry the remaining two tribes of Judah into captivity. Years later God allowed a

remnant of Judah, now cured of their idolatrous worship, to return to Palestine.

4. Persia was the next empire to rule the world. Here Satan instigated Haman to obtain a decree from the king ordering the massacre of every Jew throughout this vast empire. In the Book of Esther one reads of Israel's fantastic deliverance through a miraculous chain of events, all supernaturally timed.

5. The Grecian Empire was divided among Alexander's generals after his early death. Over the greatest of these divisions, in the course of time, ruled Antiochus Epiphanes. This king was completely under Satan's power. He was determined to kill every Jew who refused to give up his religion and distinctiveness. Once again Satan would have cut the Messianic line if God had not raised up the courageous Maccabees to preserve the Jewish people.

6. *One is now reigning.* Most students believe this is a clear reference to Domitian the reigning emperor. He, more than any other emperor in the first century, hated the Jews. He vented this hate in persecution. He put special taxes on them and planned a general repression of this people.

7. Who is the seventh head, the next ruler? After the fall of the Roman Empire, which ruler took up the Satanic theme, echoed through the centuries and voiced in Psalm 83:4 (KJV), "Come, and let us cut them off from being a nation; That the name of Israel may be no more in remembrance"? In the past nineteen centuries, which ruler stands head and shoulders above all the six preceeding rulers in his ability to kill Jews? Which ruler beat to death, shot, gassed, or burned 6 million Jewish men, women, children, even babies?

If one reads this horrible story, a nightmare without any equal in all the centuries of history, one must conclude that here was a ruler truly possessed by Satan. It surely seems that a human being without an inner devil could never be guilty of such heinous crimes.

Referring to this seventh ruler the apostle writes, "When he does come, he is only to last for a little while." That helps! If Hitler had won World War II, he would have killed every Jew on the face of the earth.

To many, the idea of Hitler being the seventh head is a new thought and hence painful. Doubters must read *Guide*, Appendix 43 where two truly astounding articles from *Life* Magazine are described.

If Hitler was the seventh and last head of the red beast, who will be the very next Satan-possessed ruler? John gives a clear answer: "The beast . . . is himself an eighth king . . ." (17:11 BERKELEY). The beast is not an eighth head, since there were only seven. But this red beast is an eighth king, the Antichrist of the tomorrows! The Antichrist will be more powerful than any of the seven preceeding kings, since he will possess all of Satan's power and authority (13:4).

He can be identified not only by his worldwide power but also by his godlessness and utterly blasphemous utterances (13:5-8). Is it not highly significant and understandable that he can further be identified because his color is *red?*

What nation today meets these four specifications—worldwide power, godless, utterly blasphemous, and designated as *red?* If still in doubt, Ezekiel states that this king will invade Israel from his place "... in the uttermost parts of the north" (Ezekiel 38:6; 39:2 ASV). (See chart of Day of God's Wrath.)

In the tomorrows this red beastly Antichrist will attempt to finish the genocide of his seven Satanic heads. Hence, there is a sixth reason why Russia is the most likely nation to produce the Antichrist. Today Russia indicates that she proposes to destroy Israel—the same murderous endeavor of all of her seven heads. Thus we read this typical news story in our daily papers: "Russia today announced two bold new initiatives in Middle East policy, pledging support of the overthrow of Israel." Up to this time Russia had taken a poorly veiled neutral stance. Now she takes her stand with the seven preceeding kings Satanically inspired to wipe Israel completely off the map.

There is another prediction that will clinch the identity of the red Antichrist. It has not been fulfilled yet. Daniel 9:27 refers to a treaty that the Antichrist will make with Israel. If Russia makes a treaty with Israel, then the stack of identifying evidences becomes almost conclusive. Then if Russia breaks the treaty after 3½ years, prohibits the Israelis from worshipping in their new temple, and substitutes some abominable idol there—the evidence is absolutely conclusive (Daniel 9:27; Matthew 24:15; 2 Thessalonians 2:3-6).

Only Christians who know these predictions will be able to discern these times and be able to intelligently avoid their pitfalls! Here is the helpful reason why the Lord made these predictions.

Three times (twice in verse 8 and once in verse 11) John stresses most unusual facts about the beastly Antichrist:

> The beast you have seen is he who once was alive, and is
> alive no longer, but has yet to ascend out of the abyss . . .
> (Revelation 17:8 NEB).

Isn't that strange? The Antichrist was not alive in the first century but he had been alive at some previous time. Will that man be resurrected at some future date to become the Antichrist? That answer in a moment!

In an earlier chapter John states that one of the fallen five kings will "recover from his mortal wound" (13:3). One immediately wonders how one of these five dead kings could be brought to life to become the future Antichrist!

One of these five dead kings was Antiochus Epiphanes who was the mirrored image of the Antichrist of the future. Both Antiochus and the Antichrist are fiendishly dedicated to destroy Israel; both prohibit the worship of Jehovah in the temple and substitute an abominable idol; and both persecute the Jews for the same period of time—3½ years.

Will the Antichrist be a resurrected Antiochus? I do not think so. A parallel exists in Scripture. The prophet Malachi predicted that the dead Elijah would return before Christ (Malachi 4:5). But Elijah was not resurrected before Jesus came. Speaking of His forerunner, John the Baptist, Jesus explained that John ". . . himself is Elijah who was to come" (Matthew 11:14 BERKELEY). John came in the same spirit of Elijah and was similar in other ways. Just as John the Baptist was the forerunner of Christ, preaching the same gospel (Matthew 3:2; 4:17), similarily, Antiochus was the forerunner of the Antichrist, both much alike in several ways.

Not only did the *red* beast have seven heads but he also had ten horns. John explains the meaning of these ten horns:

> His ten horns are ten kings who have not yet risen to power; they will be appointed to their kingdoms for one brief moment, to reign with him.
> They will all sign a treaty giving their power and strength to him.
> Together they will wage war against the Lamb, and the Lamb will conquer them; for He is Lord over all lords, and King of kings, and His people are the called and chosen and faithful ones. (Revelation 17:12–14 LNT)

Ten kings who have not yet risen to power. Both Daniel and John give the *time* period of these ten kings as the *time* of the future return of Christ who will then destroy them (Daniel 2:34,35,45; 7:7–14,24–27; Revelation 17:12–14).

Comparison of these passages will thrill the reader with the glorious unity and inspiration of the Bible! The activity of these ten kings, as both Daniel and John declare, is still future in our day.

Previous reference to Revelation 17:16 indicated that the ten kings and the Antichrist will hate the harlot and burn her with fire. There one also noted that the woman is sitting on the beastly Antichrist who is fortified with ten horns. What the harlot sits on, she tries to control with rein and spur. Naturally, red Russia and her allies will hate the directives of the harlot and will destroy her, as the Bible predicts.

Who are these ten kings? Ideologically they belong to red Russia. Yet they must have a strong Catholic element in them. Since the Yalta Conference, when Russia wormed its way into control of Poland and the Catholic nations of East Europe, Catholicism and Communism have been fighting stealthily for the domination of these countries.

The ten kings will all sign a treaty giving their power and strength to him (the Antichrist). Even today, the Warsaw Treaty Organization has seven member nations. Within this high iron fence, Russia has corralled and locked these cowed allies: Poland, East Germany, Czechoslovakia, Hungary, Bulgaria, and Rumania. Secret treaties with other neighboring countries could exist. In 1969 when Czechoslovakia tried to crash the gate, the world realized that this treaty organization was brittle. Daniel referred to these ten kings of the Antichrist as ten toes composed of a friable mixture of iron and clay (Daniel 2:41–45). What an accurate prediction of the weakness of Russia and her balky allies in East Europe.

When will Russia and her ten allies destroy the harlot (Revelation 17:16)? John Walvoord is one scholar who believes the Antichrist will destroy Rome at the beginning of the Tribulation. He feels the Antichrist will not need her help any longer. The Antichrist will want the undivided worship of the world for himself.

On the other hand, J.B. Smith believes Rome will be burned with fire very close to the end of the Tribulation. Since Vatican City is in the city of Rome, surrounded by it, it is logical that the two will be burned at the same time. The burning of Babylon [Rome] occurs at the close of the Tribulation (Revelation 14:8; 16:19; 18:2,10,21).

Furthermore, it has been the history of Catholicism throughout the centuries to *adapt* to any distasteful situation that has threatened her existence. Since the Antichrist will have significant opposition even to the close of the Tribulation (Revelation 9:16, Daniel 11:44), he may find Rome useful to him as long as the Vatican remains silent.

One should carefully read dramatic Revelation 18, detailing the destruction of Rome. One discovers that as Rome burns, the Lord has not yet split the skies to return to this earth. This fact is evident as the onlookers of the burning are not crying to God for mercy but are lamenting the loss of their business relations with Rome (18:9–19). Their lament takes up about half the chapter. Things of this earth still fill all their horizons!

John may have remembered that days were required to burn only a part of Nero's Rome. Yet faithful recorder John wrote that Rome will be "utterly burned with fire" in *one day*. Almost immediately he repeatedly adds that the city will be destroyed in *one hour* (18:10,17,19 KJV).

Such talk was sensational in John's day. And in our day, too—until the discovery of the atomic bomb! One small hydrogen bomb could do everything predicted in this chapter. Yes, in a single hour!

Why did the captains of ships out at sea stand afar off "fearing danger to themselves"? Even on land curious people go fairly close to a burning building. Twice John emphasizes that even the ships at sea "stand a long way off" (18:15,17). Do the actions of these future sailors make sense?

As one reads in Revelation 18 about the great importance of the Rome of the end of this age, one wonders if the Rome of our day is due for a vast expansion. Perhaps it is great because the much greater cities of today have all vanished in the dust of coming nuclear explosions. One cannot be sure.

If one considers it to be a description of papal Rome in Revelation 17, he will be impressed by its close similarity to the city of Rome in Revelation 18: (1) Same symbolic name, *Babylon* (17:5: 18:2,10,21); (2) Same expensive adornment (17:4; 18:16); (3) Same conniving with secular rulers (17:1,2,15; 18:3,9); (4) Same persecution of God's people (17:6; 18:20,24); (5) Same worldwide influence (17:1,2,15,18; 18:3,9,24); (6) Same doom of burning with fire (17:16; 18:8,9,18).

The proximity and close association of papal Rome and the city of Rome accounts for the marked similarity. The two are twins, one specializing in religion, the other in commerce.

What nations will destroy Rome? John is told the answer:

> . . . As for the ten horns you saw, they together with the beast will come to hate the whore; they . . . will burn her to ashes. For God has put it into their heads to carry out his purpose, by making common cause and conferring their sovereignty upon the beast until all that God has spoken is fulfilled. The woman you saw is the great city that holds sway over the kings of the earth. (17:16–18 NEB)

Divine permission for the wicked to destroy the wicked is very common throughout the Bible. Note the red Beast (the Antichrist) destroys Rome, whose sins have been described. These verses should convince the diehards that the Antichrist is not the head of a resurrected Roman Empire with his capital at Rome. It is preposterous that he should destroy himself. His destruction will be taken up in later chapters.

Henry Alford saw things clearly as he wrote this in *The Greek New Testament:*

> . . . They [the seven heads] belong to the beast, which is not Rome nor the Roman Empire but a general symbol of secular anti-Christian power.

The next chapter describes heaven's glorious wedding-supper—that blessed day when Christ is united with His bride the Church. One moment here will repay for all the trials of life!

23

THE VICTORIOUS CLIMAX

Revelation 19

Revelation 19 gives the climactic events at the very end of this age. This is the first:

> After this I heard what sounded like the voice of a great throng in heaven that said, "Hallelujah! The salvation, the glory and the power belong to God, because His judgments are true and just. For He has sentenced the great harlot, who corrupted the earth with her lewdness, and He has required from her hand retribution for the blood of His servants." And a second time they shouted "Hallelujah! And her smoke shall ascend forever and ever." (19:1–3 BERKELEY)

Here one sees the redeemed in heaven. At long last the Lord had resurrected the dead in Christ and gathered them with the living Christians into heaven—an event called the Rapture. Before taking up the glories in heaven, they seem to look back to earth at the burning of Rome. They proclaim that God's action against Rome is true and just. These remarks seem to indicate that the time of the Rapture coincides somewhat with the time of the burning of Rome.

This view is confirmed by the next verses, stating that this is the wedding day of Christ with His church. These facts invalidate the view of some who state that the Rapture took place seven years before the burning of Rome and this union of Christ with His bride.

The rejoicing of the Christians in heaven is not carnal but stems from a heavenly voice speaking to them.

> Celebrate over her, O heaven, and you saints and apostles and prophets, for on your behalf God has decided sentence against her. (18:20 Berkeley)

On your behalf. For the first three centuries of the Christian era, political Rome was the persecutor of Jew and Christian. But from the fourth century to the present, papal Rome in its persecution far exceeded its predecessor.

Both political Rome and papal Rome have the same symbolic name. Both destroy God's people and both will be destroyed by fire (17:1,16,18; 18:8,20,21; 19:2). A study of these passages with their contexts indicates that they are destroyed at the same time.

His judgments are true and just. This verdict is repeatedly stated (15:3; 16:7; 19:2,11). The martyrs who suffered unspeakable tortures and often death over a slowly burning fire ought to know. Also proclaiming that God's judgments are just is the angel who saw the rivers of the world reddened with the blood of the martyrs (16:5). Armchair theorists of today will criticize God's judgments on wicked Rome as being brutish, but not the millions who had firsthand knowledge of Rome's heinous tortures.

Hallelujah! This Hebrew word has been carried into English in the New Testament without being translated. All of its four occurrences in the New Testament are found in this chapter: verses 1,3,4,6. In the Old Testament it is found often in the later Psalms but there it is always translated into English as "Praise ye the Lord."

Hallelujah is the exulting exclamation of the martyrs who now see the triumph of God in a world that thought God was dead. Now with the burning of the world's greatest persecutor, Rome, they praise God that he has finally bared His mighty right arm. They rejoice not because wicked people are dying but because an evil worldwide system is destroyed.

Who burns Rome? The red Antichrist with his ten allies burn papal Rome (17:16). If one studies 18:20 through 19:3 he gets the impression that papal Rome and the city of Rome are burned at the same time. If that is true then the Antichrist burns the city of Rome. In that case the Antichrist will not head up a future Roman Empire as some older commentators taught.

After their backward look at Rome, the redeemed now give their attention to their heavenly surroundings:

Then the twenty-four elders and the four living beings fell down to worship God, who is seated upon the throne, exclaiming, "Amen! Hallelujah!" And a voice came forth from the throne that said, "Render praise to our God, all His servants who revere Him, both small and great!"

And I then heard, like the voice of a mighty throng, like the sound of many waters, like the roar of terrific thunders, "Hallelujah, for the Lord our God, the Omnipotent has become sovereign King." (19:4–6 BERKELEY)

Like the voice of a mighty throng, like the sound of many waters, like the roar of terrific thunder. The awed apostle heaps up his strongest similes! Words will be totally inadequate to express what the Christian will see, hear, and feel when he gets to heaven. The redeemed are overwhelmed with ecstatic joy at the prospect of having their wonderful Saviour at the head of world government.

John had previously heard "strong shoutings" in heaven when the seventh trumpet blew:

. . . We give Thee thanks, Lord God Almighty . . . because Thou hast assumed Thy great power and hast taken sovereign charge. (11:17 BERKELEY)

The enchanted saints have another reason for their jubilance:

. . . Let us rejoice, let us be glad with all our hearts. Let us give him glory, for the wedding day of the Lamb has come, and His bride has made herself ready. She may be seen dressed in linen, gleaming and spotless—for such linen is the righteous living of the saints.

Then He said to me,

"Write this down: Happy are those who are invited to the wedding feast of the Lamb!"

Then he added,

"These are the true words of God." (19:7–9 PHILLIPS)

In the Old Testament Israel is portrayed as the wife of Jehovah (Isaiah 54:5; Jeremiah 31:32; Hosea 2:16). In the New Testament the Church is seen as the Bride of Christ (2 Corinthians 11:2; Ephesians 5:25–27).

The wedding day of the Lamb has come. This is the union of Christ with His church. This union occurs when Christ raises the righteous dead and gathers all Christians to heaven. It is followed by "the wed-

157

ding feast," verse 9, probably at once. It is the time for "reward to be given to thy servants, the prophets and the saints . . . (11:18 PHILLIPS). One moment at this banquet will be worth the trials of a lifetime. Observe that the timing of all of these events is close to but before the day of wrath.

His bride has made herself ready . . . dressed in linen, gleaming and spotless . . . for such linen is the righteous living of the saints. This spotless bride is a marked contrast to the harlot church, glaringly faithless to Christ. The harlot church hated the true church, only adorned with "the unfading loveliness of a calm and gentle spirit, a thing very precious in the eyes of God" (1 Peter 3:4 PHILLIPS).

The harlot church hated the true church so much and martyred so many that she became sadistically "drunk with the blood of the saints" (Revelation 17:6).

Then he said to me, "Write this down." This is one of the twelve times that John is reminded to write down what he sees and hears. Once he is told, "Write not." These thirteen directives remind one of the opening statement of this prophecy, "This is a Revelation from Jesus Christ" (1:1).

These are the true words of God. This book is not a compilation of writings from prophetic and inspired writers but it contains "the true words of God." What holy ground! How carefully and reverently one should study this book, unique from all other books of the Bible!

If following these "true words of God" should lead one to a firing squad or gas chamber, he should certainly march there triumphantly.

John was so impressed by the angel who spoke God's words that he wrote this about it:

> Then I fell down at his feet to worship him, but he said, "No! Don't! For I am a servant of God just as you are, and as your brother Christians are, who testify of their faith in Jesus. The purpose of all prophecy and of all that I have shown you is to tell about Jesus." (19:10 LNT)

It is not exhilarating to remember that those "who testify of their faith in Jesus" have ambassador status not one whit below any angelic messenger in heaven? Men and angels exist to serve and obey God, never to set themselves on any pedestal to be worshipped. God's anointed and highest cherub forgot that once and made all creation to be cursed (Ezekiel 28:14–19).

Adhere to their witnessing for Jesus (Berkeley). Revelation never minimizes the danger of witnessing for Jesus (Revelation 6:9; 11:7; 12:17; 20:4) but it also warns of the much greater suffering and eternal loss by conforming to the standards of this world (14:10,11; 20:12–15; 21:8). Much better to be martyred than to suffer the wrath of God!

The apostle now describes the wrath of God. Remember that the Bride of Christ has been gathered out of the world before God's wrath is poured.

> Then I saw Heaven wide open, and before my eyes appeared a white horse, whose rider is called faithful and true, for His judgment and His warfare are just. His eyes are a flame of fire and there are many diadems upon His head. There is a name written upon him, known only to himself. He is dressed in a cloak dipped in blood, and the name by which He is known is the Word of God.
>
> The armies of Heaven follow him, riding upon white horses and clad in white and spotless linen. Out of his mouth there comes a sharp sword with which to strike the nations. He will shepherd them "with a rod of iron," and alone He will tread the winepress of the furious wrath of God the Almighty. Written upon his cloak and upon his thigh is the name, KING OF KINGS AND LORD OF LORDS. (19:11–16 PHILLIPS)

Here begins the description of the day of God's wrath, depicted by many prophets. This day will begin when the seventh angel sounds his trumpet (11:15–19). But the Rapture will occur just *before* the last trumpet actually sounds (10:7; 1 Corinthians 15:52).

Then I saw Heaven wide open. An open heaven or open temple is one of the hallmarks of the day of wrath (Revelation 6:14; 11:19). Isaiah yearned for this day to correct the wickedness in the world:

> Oh for the heavens to rend,
> > oh for thee to descend . . .
> to let thy foes know what thou
> > art,
> > till the world trembles at thy
> > presence. . . .
> > > > (Isaiah 64:1,2 MOFFATT)

A white horse, whose rider is called Faithful and True . . . the Word of God . . . King of Kings and Lord of Lords. Here are five names denoting the deity of Jesus Christ. What a contrast to the nameless rider of the white horse of Revelation 6! The white horse rider of Revelation 6 (the United Nations?) is today conniving to bring the Soviet variety of peace on the earth. But he will fail and be displaced by the rider on the red horse and a frightful war killing one-fourth of the earth's people (6:8).

But the rider of Revelation 19 will destroy those who are devastating the earth and then set up a reign of righteousness and peace. Consider how the Lord will do this.

He is dressed in a cloak dipped in blood. . . . alone He will tread the winepress of the furious wrath of God the Almighty. Others, too, have likened this huge slaughter to a winepress (Isaiah 63:1–3; Joel 3:13; Revelation 14:19,20).

Here is Isaiah's description:

> Who comes here, all crim-
> soned,
> his robes redder than the
> vintage? . . .
> Why so red your robes,
> stained red like a vintager's?
>
> "All alone I trod the winepress,
> for no nation lent me aid;
> so I trod the foe in fury,
> trampled them down in my
> anger;
> 'twas their blood splashed my
> robes,
> till all my clothes are stained.
>
> (Isaiah 63:1–3 MOFFATT)

The armies of heaven follow Him. The armies are the countless millions of powerful angels captained by Michael the archangel (Revelation 12:7). Included also are tens of thousands of His saints (1 Thessalonians 3:13; Jude 14,15).

Out of His mouth there comes a sharp sword with which to strike the nations. Is this sword the Word of God, sharper than any two-edged sword (Hebrews 4:12)? Will He quote it to convict the wicked? One cannot be sure. However, one reads that God will panic the armies who will then destroy each other (Ezekiel 38:21; Zechariah 14:13). Does Ezekiel equate the panic with a sword?

> And I will call for a sword against him throughout all my mountains, saith the Lord God: every man's sword shall be against his brother. (Ezekial 38:21 KJV)

He will shepherd them "with a rod of iron." The rod of iron and the context connotes severity, even destruction, of offenders. Here will be a rigid execution of the law without any admixture of mercy. (Psalm 2:9; Revelation 2:27; 12:5; 19:15).

> Then I saw an angel standing alone in the blazing light of the sun, and he shouted in a loud voice, calling to all the birds flying in mid-air:
> "Come, flock together to God's great feast! Here you may eat the flesh of kings and captains, the flesh of strong men, of horses and their riders—the flesh of all men, free men and slaves, small and great!" (19:17,18 PHILLIPS)

Describing this same day, Ezekiel also notes the calling of the birds to eat the dead. In this future battle the number of the dead will be far too many for the few survivors to bury:

> . . . give this message from the Lord the Eternal to all sorts of birds and to every wild beast: "Come gather and collect from all quarters to the feast . . . that I am preparing for you, a rich feast on the uplands of Israel, where you can eat flesh and drink blood; you shall eat the flesh of heroes and drink the blood of the world's princes. . . . (Ezekiel 39:17,18 MOFFATT)

This similarity between John's and Ezekiel's descriptions is only one evidence that both prophets are portraying the same battle. Observe these additional evidences: (2) Both prophets refer to this battle as the time of God's wrath (Ezekiel 38:18–20; Revelation 19:15). (3) In both prophecies the contexts indicate that this is the *last* battle of this age. (4) Both prophets emphasize that after this conflict the whole world will recognize the sovereignty of God (Ezekiel 38:23; 39:7,21–39; Rev. 19:20; 20:1–4). (5) Both stress the godless character of Israel's invader (Ezekiel 38:14–22; Revelation 19:19).

Because of the unusual character of this last conflict and the striking similarity of these two descriptions, there should be no reasonable doubt that both prophets are describing the *same* struggle.

There is an important reason for equating Ezekiel 38 and 39 with Revelation 19. In Revelation the spotlight is on the red beast, the Antichrist, who heads up the godless forces against Christ (17:3; 19:-19,20).

In the Ezekiel passage the spotlight is also turned repeatedly on the leader of the godless allies. But in Ezekiel it is twice stated that this ruler invades Israel from his country "in the uttermost parts of the north" (38:6; 39:2 ASV).

Isn't that helpful? Since both Ezekiel and John had the same battle and the same godless ruler in mind, cannot one logically conclude that the red beast of Revelation, the Antichrist, invades Israel from "the uttermost parts of the north"?

Does the concept of Russia invading Israel seem like a most bizarre and unlikely possibility today? Quite the reverse! In fact, most nations are alarmed because this probability is increasing very rapidly. They fear this conflict will mean another world war with all the ugly overtones of nuclear destruction. Perhaps these predictions of the prophets were vague and meaningless through the centuries but certainly today they bristle with certainty.

Today the only threat that Israel fears lives "in the uttermost parts of the north"—Red Russia! The Arab nations are only puppets of Russia and in themselves pose no real threat to Israel.

Ezekiel not only pinpointed the country invading Israel in the tomorrows, but gave the approximate time of the invasion:

> After many days . . . in the latter years . . . the land . . . that is gathered out of many peoples upon the mountains of Israel, which have been a continual waste. . . . against the waste places that are now inhabited, and against the people that are gathered out of the nations. . . . (Ezekiel 38:8,12 ASV)

This prophecy could not have been fulfilled before 1948 because Israel was not a nation "gathered out of the nations." Neither did Russia threaten her before that date. However, shortly after Israel became an independent nation (1948), Russia discovered that Israel refused to become a red puppet. It was then that Russia took an active role in arming and encouraging the Arab nations to destroy Israel. But the Arabs repeatedly met with miraculous and stinging defeats, much to Russia's chagrin.

In 1970 Russia cast off her thinly disguised neutrality and publicly declared that Israel must be destroyed. It has been reported that Russia has thousands of military personnel and Soviet pilots flying Russian jets in Egypt.

Might Russia invade Israel any day? Before Russia invades Israel for the last battle of this age, one prediction of Ezekiel must be fulfilled. At the time of this invasion, Ezekiel predicted a tranquility in Israel that certainly does not exist today:

> . . . the land that has recovered from war and is occupied by
> people, now living in security, all of them. . . . (Ezekiel 38:8
> BERKELEY)

Today Israel is fighting a limited undeclared war with Jordan, Syria,
Lebanon, Iraq, and Egypt. She certainly is not "recovered from war
and . . . now living in security."

How will this peace and security be achieved? Nobody can be sure.
However, Daniel predicts that Israel will make a treaty with the Antichrist, who will break it after 3½ years (Daniel 9:27). During that
time Israel should certainly have security and peace. Israel, in order
to survive, may be forced into such a treaty, if the United States fails
to sell her the jets and other needed military equipment. Furthermore,
in Israel there are some doves and leftists who are pressuring the
government to negotiate with Russia.

Now back to Revelation 19 to discover the result of the battle between the godless nations at Armageddon and the Rider on the white
horse:

> Then I saw the beast [the Antichrist] and the kings of the
> earth and their armies mustered to do battle with the Rider
> and his army. The beast was taken prisoner, and so was the
> false prophet who had worked miracles in its presence and
> deluded those who had received the mark of the beast and
> worshipped its image. The two of them were thrown alive
> into the lake of fire with its sulphurous flames. The rest were
> killed by the sword which went out of the Rider's mouth; and
> all the birds gorged themselves on their flesh. (19:19-21 NEB)

24

THE GREAT DAY OF GOD'S WRATH

The great day of God's wrath is one of the most important subjects
in the Bible, yet, sadly misunderstood! To be sure, this topic is tucked
away in widely separated Scriptures and has been rarely gathered and
studied as a unit.

If one does ferret out these passages and unifies them, he will enter a new dimension in understanding many obscure areas of the Word. He will be pleasantly surprised to discover that these references are very relevant in discerning these bewildering times.

Scholars who have harmonized the four gospel records have rendered a great service. Only when the four gospels are arranged chronologically in parallel columns can one readily study the order of events in the life of our Lord.

Similarily, this writer now seeks to unify those portions of Scriptures depicting the day of wrath. When one fits these pieces together he can readily see an informative picture of this great day.

In Revelation 16 the first six bowls contain divine wrath against the Antichrist and his country *during the Tribulation.* Only the seventh bowl describes the final great day of God's wrath. Jesus drew a clear line of demarcation between the Great Tribulation and the great day of God's wrath (Matthew 24:29).

Prophets call the last day of this age "the great day of His wrath" (Revelation 6:17) or "the day of vengeance" (Isaiah 61:2) or very often "the day of the Lord" (Joel 3:14). The finding of such names along with certain most unusual catastrophic events should label that Scripture as a description of this great day of God's wrath.

A Scripture possessing these criteria is Revelation 6:12–17, PHILLIPS translation. Here are cataclysmic events that set this day apart from all other days, even those of the Great Tribulation (Revelation 8 and 9). It is most unlikely that this age will ever witness another such day.

One knows that Isaiah, Joel, and Jesus also describe this *identical* day because they list these same unusual never-to-be-repeated phenomena. Jesus' description of this day is very similar to John's, yet He adds distinctive details. (See Matthew 24:29,30 KJV.)

Jesus puts a definite time tag on this day of wrath as "immediately after the tribulation." Many students fail to note this fact, perhaps because He is the only One who makes the timing crystal clear.

On the chart shown here are ten Scriptures portraying this outstanding day. They are listed on the top horizontal line. (For a more complete list see Guide, Appendix 44.)

On the top of the left column, note the first item— *WHAT.* The Day of Wrath is a description of the final event of this age: the destruction of the wicked. Observe that nine of the ten references are bound together by this most unusual portrayal.

In the left vertical column of the chart, consider the unusual catastrophic events listed there: open heaven, falling stars (meteorites), darkened sun, reddened moon, punishment of all the wicked nations and their recognition of the sovereignty of God. This bizarre combination of phenomena will never be seen again in this age.

THE GREAT DAY OF GOD'S WRATH

	Matt. 24: 29,30	Rev. 6: 12-17	Rev. 11: 15-19	Rev. 14: 10-20	Rev. 16: 17-21	Rev. 19: 11-21	Isa. 13: 9-13	Eze. 38 & 39	Joel 2 & 3	Zech. 12-14
WHAT: Destruction of wicked		Rev. 6: 15-17	Rev. 11: 18	Rev. 14: 14-20	Rev. 16: 19	Rev. 19: 15-18	Isa. 13: 9	Eze. 38: 22-28; 39:3-20	3:2-13	14:3,12
WHEN:	Just after the Tribulation	Sixth Seal	Seventh Trumpet	Return of Christ	Seventh Bowl	Return of Christ	Day of the Lord	After Israel's Return	Day of the Lord	Day of the Lord
WHERE:								Israel	Israel 3:2,12	Israel
WHO:				Beast 14:11	Armageddon, v. 16	Beast 19:19,20		Gog from Rosh. 38:2,18 39:1,11		
HOW: 1. Heaven or temple opened		6:14	11:19		16:17	19:11			2:10 3:16	
2. Earth or heaven shaken	Matt. 24: 29	6:12	11:19		16:18		13:13	38:19,20	2:10 3:15	14:4,5
3. Stars fall	24:29	6:13					13:10			
4. Sun darkened	24:29	6:12					13:10		2:10,31 3:15	
5. Moon dark or reddened	24:29	6:12					13:10		2:10,31 3:15	
6. Thunder and lightning			11:19		16:18			38:22		
7. Hailstones			11:19		16:21					
AFTERMATH: 1. Slaughter like a winepress;				14:19,20		19:15			3:13	
2. Like a harvest with a scythe				14:19-20					3:13	
3. Slain are many—scavengers required						19:17-21		39:17-21		
4. All nations recognize sovereignty of God	24:30	6:17	11:15			19:15		38:23 39:7,21		14:9,16

Hence, one can reasonably conclude that all of these ten Scriptures are depicting the same day. It is important to engrave this fact on the mind.

Some of these passages contain important details not found in the others. To illustrate take the second item in the left column, *WHEN.* Mention has been made that only Jesus gives the time of the Day of Wrath in the Matthew 24:29 reference, "immediately after the tribulation." Since all of these passages describe the *same* day, one can put Jesus' time tag on all the other Scriptures. Ability to put this precise time tag on these passages enlarges the meaning and greatly helps in the interpretation.

Ezekiel 38:8 puts an exciting time tag on this invasion. He states that it will occur *after* Israel has been gathered back from the many nations where they had been gathered. And to think that this return took place as recently as 1948! Does that put you in the tiptoe of expectancy? But note the last part of that verse states that at the time of the invasion, Israel will be "living all undisturbed" (MOFFATT). We suspect that this tranquility will not occur until Israel makes a treaty with the treacherous Antichrist (Daniel 9:27).

The next item in the left column is *WHERE.* Note on the chart that only Revelation 16:16 lists Armageddon as the place of the battle. Joel cites the Valley of Jehoshaphat in Israel but scholars today are uncertain of the location intended. Ezekiel and Zechariah also give the place as Israel but they, too, lack the specificity of the Revelation reference. Ability to apply these specifics as to time and place are of inestimable value in a full orbed interpretation.

Particularly is that true in taking up the next subject in the left column, *WHO.* Who is this final invader of Israel? Fortunately Ezekiel names this godless invader and pinpoints his country—". . . Gog, the prince of Rosh and Meshech and Tubal" who comes from Magog (Ezekiel 38:2 MOFFATT). For many centuries scholars have associated Rosh, Meshech, and Tubal with Red Russia and its cities. (See *Guide,* Appendix 45 for intriguing details.) Dr. Wilbur Smith in *World Crises and the Prophetic Scriptures* quotes from ancient sources to show that Russia obtained its very name from "Rosh" in the Ezekiel passage just quoted.

Such historical research is confirmatory, yet one really does not need it to determine the origin of *Gog, Prince of Rosh.* As mentioned previously, three times Ezekiel states that this ruler of an anti-God confederacy comes into Israel from "the uttermost parts of the north" (Ezekiel 38:6,15; 39:2 ASV and RSV).

In the previous chapter five reasons were given to show that Ezekiel

38 and 39 are describing the same conflict depicted in Revelation 19. If one also observes the common denominators that these Scriptures have on the chart, he must come to the same conclusion that they are portraying the same time and the same battle.

If Ezekiel and John had the same conflict in mind, it seems logical that they were describing the same conspicuous leader of the godless confederacy of nations, the same target of divine wrath. What point am I trying to make? If Ezekiel conclusively shows that the godless ruler of the anti-God forces comes from Red Russia, then is it not logical to conclude that the godless ruler described by John must also come from Russia?

Karl Marx in his writings laid the foundation for Russia's godlessness. When asked for the purpose of his life, Marx replied, "To overthrow God!" Would any sane individual make such a statement without being possessed by the red Devil? It was Satan who voiced a similar statement centuries before (Isaiah 14:13,14).

Expressing the plan of the Russian Revolution, Zenovieff boasted, "We will grapple with the Lord God in due season; we shall vanquish him in his highest heaven, and wherever he seeks refuge, and we shall subdue him forever."

Molder of young people and former Russian Commissar of Education, Anatole Lunarcharsky declared:

> We hate Christians and Christianity. Even the best of them must be considered our worst enemies. They preach love of one's neighbor and mercy, which is contrary to our principles. *Christian love is an obstacle to the development of the Revolution.*

After being brainwashed with such teaching daily and for fifty some years, Russia is perfectly conditioned to do what the Bible predicts—*worship the Devil himself* for giving their own red ruler worldwide control of the nations (Revelation 13:4).

In addition to being unbelievably blasphemous there is another reason why Russia is peculiarly suited to produce the red Antichrist.

Red is the Biblical symbol for a massive slaughter (Revelation 6:4, the red horse rider with the huge sword). Repeatedly one observes that an indwelling Satan or demon in a person is suicidal or homocidal (1 Samuel 16:14; 18:10,11; 31:4; Matthew 4:5,6; 8:28–32; 27:5; John 13:27; Luke 9:39; Acts 19:14–16). No wonder that Jesus speaking of the Devil said, "... He was a murderer from the beginning ..." (John 8:44). From the incitation of Cain to murder, the Devil and his demons have been dedicated to killing people. The Devil surely deserves the stigma of being red.

Modern psychiatry also recognizes that man has within him a murderous force called "the death instinct." Psychiatrists also recognize an opposing force called "the life instinct." (For elaboration see *Guide*, Appendix 22.)

Naturally, the red Devil infuses the red Antichrist with his killing instincts. Hence, the Antichrist will redden the world with the blood "of a great multitude which no man could number" (Revelation 7:9). Their only crime was witnessing for Christ. It is understandable why the Scripture calls the Antichrist a "scarlet coloured Beast" (17:3).

Is Russia qualified above other nations to produce a murderous ruler? Karl Marx, who tattooed the Russian planners with murderous designs, explained in *The Civil War in France* the error of the proletariat, ". . . instead of annihilating its enemies, it endeavored to exercise moral influence on them."

When Lenin overthrew Russia's shortlived democracy (January 18, 1918), he followed from the start the ideas of Marx. In the civil war that he initiated, 28 million Russians perished, according to W. Cleon Skousen in *The Naked Communist.*

Even that astronomical figure was dwarfed when the brutal Stalin and his hatchet man Khrushchev entered the world stage. With their connivings and unbelievable massacres in the countries of eastern Europe, China, Korea, and Southeast Asia, many tens of millions perished. The methods used by Stalin to paint China red and the enormous massacres that followed—these can only be described by one big red word, *diabolical.*

With Russia playing the major role in the shaping and painting of the world in the seventies, every person who wants to discern these days, should certainly read at least a summary of events in the decade of the forties. (See *Guide*, Appendix 25 for full background.)

If he does, one fact screams for attention. No nation has ever been responsible for shedding as much red blood within its own borders and around the world as Red Russia.

For years Russians have been conditioned to think of killing every time they look at their red flag: "The red represents the blood that will have to be shed to bring the revolution to the world," as the guide told Billy Graham. Their leaders have repeatedly and publicly boasted that their aim is world revolution and control.

And the Bible repeatedly predicts that a blasphemous slaughterous red Antichrist will do just that. What country stands the best chance to accomplish this task?

For centuries Ezekiel's prediction that Russia would invade Israel "in the latter years" seemed utterly groundless—but not in the seventies. Israel's military idol, General Moshe Dayan, stated in 1968, "The next war will not be with the Arabs but with the Russians." In that year the Israelis assured me, "It is not the Arabs we fear. It is Russia."

In 1970 the Soviets built extensive missile sites in Egypt, manned by Russian military experts. Soviet pilots flying the latest in Russian planes are poised ready to blow the Israelis to bits. Today nobody ridicules Ezekiel's prophecy!

A theological professor asked me recently how long historians and anthropologists have known that Ezekiel's "land of Magog" is the land now occupied by the USSR. From the fifth century B.C. (See *Guide*, Appendix 45 for a fuller review of this subject.)

However, the idea of clumsy backward Russia ever heading a vast confederacy of nations did seem absurd—until the middle of this century. Just how, within a few decades, this nation became the powerful worldwide Frankenstein monster that she is today is explained in *Guide*, Appendix 46.

Now to the left column of the chart titled "The Great Day of God's Wrath," and the word *HOW*. The armies of the world will gather in Israel to capture Jerusalem (Zechariah 12:3). Since it wouldn't take all the armies to capture one city, there must be two or more opposing groups wanting Israel, vital to the control of the vast oil and other resources in the Middle East (Zechariah 12:2,3; Daniel 11:41,45). The allies of the Antichrist are there and opposing them is a vast army of 200 million from the Far East (Revelation 9:16).

Awaiting this monstrous confederacy at Armageddon are the allies of the Antichrist, now resting after their devastation of Israel. About the time the confrontation occurs between Russia and China and their allies, the Lord splits the skies to avenge the devastation of Jerusalem and Israel (Zechariah 12:9; 14:2,3).

John F. Walvoord writes about this in *The Revelation of Jesus Christ*.

> . . . with the appearance of the Lord in glory and the procession of the armies of heaven accompanying Him, these armies of earth forget their differences and join in battle against the King of kings and Lord of lords.

Satan knows it is his only chance and takes it (Psalm 2; Revelation 19:19). He has fought with God before and lost (12:7–9). But now impressed with the armies and their vast stockpiles of nuclear and other weapons, he hopes for victory.

Then God sends the world's greatest earthquake (16:18), falling "stars," dense darkness, a red moon, lightning, thunder, and hailstones.

Of course, the armies panic. In their terror they mistake friends for foes and let fly every weapon they possess (Ezekiel 38:21; Zechariah 14:13). How much like the victory that Gideon won (Judges 7:22).

Observe on the chart how the prophets describe varied aspects of the great *AFTERMATH* of this day. As was brought out previously, some prophets liken the immensity of the slaughter to the red wine from a winepress. One adds that "the blood gushed out of the winepress as high as a horse's bridle" (14:20). Other prophets likened the slain to the grain cut by the scythes. Others sought to show the unbelievable mortality by calling for the birds and wild beasts to eat the bodies—far, far too many to bury.

The bottom line of the chart emphasizes the most significant result of this great day—all nations recognize the sovereignty of the Lord Jesus Christ. Such international acknowledgment indicates that all of these Scriptures on the chart are describing the final day of this age. In the Tribulation period (Revelation 8,9,12,13), Satan seemed to be in control. But when the Lord returns in power and glory, all will bow to Him.

Putting the facts from these ten Scriptures on the chart is like the feeding of data into a computer. After this basic task is done, one can go to the chart to obtain answers to many perplexing questions. Here are some of the computerized conclusions:

1. A glance at the second horizontal line reveals that the sixth seal, the seventh trumpet, the seventh bowl and the return of Christ occur at the *same* time. This fact gives inestimable help in determining the chronology of the Revelation as well as its interpretation.

2. Jesus stated that the events in the left vertical column (day of God's wrath), occur "immediately after the Tribulation" (Matthew 24:29). Hence, the Great Tribulation and the day of God's wrath are two distinct periods. Many writers fail to make this distinction. As a result, they teach a pre-tribulation Rapture instead of a pre-wrath Rapture. President of Gordon-Conwell Seminary Harold J. Ockenga clearly sees this important distinction.

3. Some writers have difficulty putting a time tag on Ezekiel 38 and 39. These chapters have so many common denominators with the Scriptures on the chart, that one is forced to conclude that Ezekiel is describing the final conflict of this age. Furthermore, Ezekiel clearly indicates that this is the last battle in Israel (Ezekiel 39:21–29), just as Armageddon is the last one in this age.

4. In Revelation 19 the target of God's wrath is the red Beast, the Antichrist. In Ezekiel 38 and 39 the main target is "Gog, prince of Rosh" coming from "the uttermost parts of the north." From this equation and the other evidences given in this chapter, can one believe that the Beast (Antichrist) will arise from Red Russia? Yet even here one should keep his conclusions fluid, in case international events change radically.

5. The study of the remarkable unity of the ten passages on the chart should thrill one with the miraculous unity and inspiration of God's Word. Devoid of all the hallmarks of copyism, such a unity manifested by writers separated by centuries of time should confirm one's faith, even if it should be tested by "dungeon, fire and sword."

With such wonderful confirmation of one's faith from God's Word, he should never be depressed by the current high tide of terrorism, violence, looting, burning, earthquakes, wars, threat of nuclear extinction, and most pathetic of all, the apostasy in the church. Depressed? Quite the contrary! Jesus and the apostles predicted that these frightening events would precede His return to catch away His Bride. Jesus advises all to take this attitude:

> But when these things occur, straighten up and lift up your heads because your deliverance is near. (Luke 21:28 BERKE-LEY)

The darker the days, the more imminent His return and our deliverance—and delivery of His Bride shall be *before* His wrath is poured out on a wicked world!

25

THE MILLENNIUM

Revelation 20

Revelation 20 gives the answers to more theological controversies than any chapter in the Bible. This chapter is also the terminus of the human activities of this age. Satan entered this world's stage in Genesis

3 but Revelation 20 depicts his exit. The clock of man's activity began in Genesis 3 but the last ticks of that clock are heard in Revelation 20.

Revelation 20 covers a period of a thousand years, usually called the Millennium (*mille* thousand; *ennium* years). Note the events at the beginning of this Millennium.

> I also saw an angel descending from heaven, holding in his hand the key of the abyss and an enormous chain. He overpowered the dragon, the serpent of old, who is the devil and Satan, and bound him for a thousand years. He hurled him into the abyss, which he shut and sealed above him, so he might lead astray the nations no more until the thousand years are completed. After that he must be released for a little while. (20:1–3 BERKELEY)

The key of the abyss. In 9:1–12 Satan was given the key to the abyss and immediately released flying agents to inflict terrible torture on the people of another country. The Bible calls that country Abyss (bottomless) to symbolize its bottomless iniquity. (For elaboration see text on Revelation 9:1–12 and *Guide*, Appendix 23.)

Since the Antichrist, a flesh and blood mortal, comes from this country (11:7), is it not logical to believe that the abyss is a nation on this earth rather than a fathomless hole in the ground? Furthermore, this country has a king as other nations have (Revelation 9:11). This king must be the Antichrist since his extremely autocratic nature, as described in Scripture, rules out his subservience to any other mortal.

Revelation 9:11 gives this psychopathic dictator the symbolic name Destroyer in both Hebrew and Greek to emphasize his Satanic compulsion to destroy. He is nihilistic. Such destruction for destruction's sake is in gear with the character of the red Antichrist (17:3) of the previous chapter.

Satan will not only be confined in this country of bottomless iniquity but he will also be locked, sealed, and securely chained there to restrict all devilish activity even in that country. If the abyss were the abode of demons, why all the efforts about locking, sealing, and chaining Satan, the logical king of demons? It just doesn't make sense!

Many wonder what human activity will be like during the Millennium. Satan and his demons will not be free to inveigle mankind. What a blessing! With Christ on the throne wars will cease. The people not killed at the battle of Armageddon will continue to go on living for some time during the Millennium. Although all will recognize the sovereignty of God and His Christ, some will chafe under the divine rule. Disobedience will bring speedy punishment. The Lord will rule with a "rod of iron" (2:27; 12:5; 19:15). Otherwise, carnality would soon ruin the wonderful blessings of this future world.

> So it shall be that all who are left from all the nations, which came up against Jerusalem, shall go up as often as once a year to worship the King, the Lord of hosts, and to celebrate the feast of booths.
>
> But if any one of the families of the earth does not go up to Jerusalem to worship the King, the Lord of hosts, there shall not be any rain upon them. (Zechariah 14:16,17 BERKELEY)

Because punishment follows quickly on the heels of disobedience, people will desist from sin. Perverseness will still exist and manifest itself occasionally in violations. But there will be no open lawlessness, no violence, no wars or blatant blasphemy of God. There will be a host of surprising blessings to make life truly wonderful. Many Scriptures give glimpses of the glories of living in the Millennium (Psalm 72; Isaiah 2:1–4; 11 and 12). Even the nature of animals is changed:

> The wolf shall live with the lamb, and the leopard shall lie down beside the kid; the calf, the young lion, and the beef cattle together, and a little child shall lead them. The cow shall graze with the bear; their young ones shall lie down together, and the lion shall eat straw like the ox.
>
> The nursing child shall play over the asp's hole, and the weaned child shall reach its hand in the snake's nest. They shall not hurt or destroy on all My holy mountain; for the earth shall be full of the knowledge of the Lord as the waters cover the sea. (Isaiah 11:6–9 BERKELEY)

Not only did John see the binding of Satan at the beginning of the Millennium, but he also saw the resurrected Christians reigning with Christ on this earth:

> Then I saw thrones, and upon them sat those to whom judgment was committed. I could see the souls of those who had been beheaded for the sake of God's word and their testimony to Jesus, those who had not worshipped the beast and its image or received its mark on forehead or hand.

These came to life again and reigned with Christ for a thousand years, though the rest of the dead did not come to life until the thousand years were over. This is the first resurrection! Happy indeed, and one of God's own people, is the man who shares in this first resurrection! Upon such the second death has no claim; but they shall be priests of God and of Christ, and shall reign with him for the thousand years. (Revelation 20:4–6 NEB)

I saw thrones and upon them sat those to whom judgment was committed. Although attention is focused on the Tribulation martyrs, one must not forget that all Christians will reign here with Christ (2 Timothy 2:12; Revelation 1:6; 5:10). One should not think it strange that Christ will return with a literal body to this earth. He left that way after living here in a body for over thirty years. Why not again as these verses so clearly state?

This is the first resurrection! Note that the "first resurrection" includes those Christians who died during the Tribulation. Hence, the first resurrection would have to be post-tribulation in time. This statement confirms the evidences previously given that the resurrection of the righteous dead will occur *after* the Tribulation. (See text of chapter 12.)

These came to life and reigned with Christ a thousand years. This resurrection occurs when the seventh or last trump "is at the point of blowing" (1 Corinthians 15:52; Revelation 10:7). The time of the Rapture is definitely pre-wrath. The church will be taken from this earth by Christ before the day of God's wrath. When the last trumpet actually blows, Christ, with His resurrected saints, will return to this earth when He will pour out divine wrath on the wicked nations gathered around Jerusalem (Revelation 11:15–19). After He defeats these, all nations will recognize His sovereignty and accept Him as King.

Revelation 20 clearly teaches that Christ will return to this earth *before* the Millennium. His return is premillennial. (See chart in chapter 8.)

Some people shut their eyes to the millennial teaching of Revelation 20, because other books do not give such a full-blown description. These critics who would downgrade chapter 20 should read the opening statement of Revelation 1:1 (NEB), "This is the Revelation given by God to Jesus Christ." From such a source, the ultimate in authority, should not one expect to receive a few *new* facts, hitherto hid from the eyes of the prophets?

Furthermore, if such critics had only accepted Revelation 20 as "the Revelation from God to Jesus Christ," they never would have had to resort to the confusion of postmillennialism and amillennialism. (For a summary of these viewpoints see *Guide,* Appendix 47.)

These reigned with Christ for a thousand years, though the rest of the dead did not come to life until the thousand years were over. This is most informative. Although both Daniel and Jesus spoke of two distinct resurrections, "the resurrection of life" and "the resurrection of damnation," only Revelation 20:4,5 specifies that the interval between these two resurrections is a thousand years.

Evidence that this is a literal period of a thousand years is presented in a most intriguing study of the number seven. All are urged to read *Guide,* Appendix 48, most relevant to the time of the Lord's return.

The Lord now reveals the events at the end of the Millennium:

> When the thousand years have ended, Satan will be released from his prison and will go out to lead astray the nations in the four quarters of the earth, Gog and Magog, to muster them for the battle. Their number is as the sand on the seashore. (Revelation 20:7,8 BERKELEY)

Satan will be released from his prison. One could hope that after meditating for a thousand years on his sins, Satan might show some fruits of repentance. Certainly God gave him enough time. But the Devil is much different from even the most wicked man. Within him there is no vestige of a divine implantation to respond to the Spirit's tug.

He will go out to lead astray the nations . . . Gog and Magog. In the preceeding chapter evidence was submitted showing that the land of the ancient Magogites is currently occupied by the Soviet Union. In the same breath describing the release of Satan from the abyss, mention is made of the country governed by Red Russia. This close association of Magog and the abyss helps to confirm previously given evidences that the abyss is a symbolic reference to Russia.

When Satan is released at the end of the Millennium, it is natural for him to turn to the same nation that headed up the anti-God forces in the great battle just before the Millennium. And logical, too! For over half a century Russia has been and still is imprinting her people with a vicious hatred against God. The deep scars of such branding will not be effaced by the centuries of the Millennium!

They surrounded the beloved city. This siege after the Millennium should not be confused with the one before. J.B. Smith in *A Revelation*

175

of Jesus Christ gives quite a few reasons to show that Ezekiel 38–39, describing the battle before the Millennium, is different from this one. He states that Gog and Magog are now names of two closely allied but separate nations. Before the Millennium Gog was the leader of the anti-God forces, after the Millennium Satan is the leader.

Their number is as the sand on the seashore. At the close of the Millennium the population of the world will be enormous. No decimations from war, famine, and pestilence! (Isaiah 2:4). All the waste places and deserts will be as fruitful as the Garden of Eden (Isaiah 51:3; 52:9; 55:12,13); life will be lengthened so that a person of a hundred years will be considered a mere child (65:20). With an omniscient and righteous Christ at the head of world government, human knowledge and economic production will reach levels inconceivable by today's concepts. Disease and death will be greatly reduced. With all the waste places productive, the enormous population explosion will offer no problems to the advanced technological skills of that day.

But smouldering in the minds of countless millions will be latent hostility against God. And when Satan and his hordes of demons are released and change these people into radicals and activists, they will welcome an opportunity to destroy the Establishment.

Satan, encouraged by these monstrous armies armed with ultramodern weapons dwarfing today's nuclear bombs, will attack Jerusalem the Golden. Observe the result:

> They marched up over the breadth of the earth and surrounded the encampment of the saints as well as the beloved city. And fire came down from heaven and consumed them. The devil, who was leading them astray, was flung into the lake of fire and sulphur where also the beast and the false prophet are, and they shall be tortured day and night forever and ever. (9–10 BERKELEY)

The devil is cast into the lake of fire where the beast and the false prophet are. These last two have been cast in at the beginning of the Millennium (19:20). They still are suffering the torments of hellfire after a thousand years and will continue to writhe in pain "day and night forever and ever." Thus Revelation 20 should settle another theological controversy—eternal punishment of the wicked.

But some will argue that only these wicked leaders and Satan will have to endure such torture. Perhaps the rest of this chapter will dispose of that question:

And then I saw a great white throne, and one seated upon it from whose presence both earth and sky fled and vanished.

Then I saw the dead, great and small, standing before the throne, and the books were opened. And another book was opened, which is the book of life. And the dead were judged by what was written in the books concerning what they had done. The sea gave up its dead, and death and the grave gave up the dead which were in them. And men were judged, each according to what he had done.

Then death and the grave were themselves hurled into the lake of fire, which is the second death. If anyone's name was not found written in the book of life he was thrown into the lake of fire. (20:11–15 PHILLIPS)

26

THE REVELATION—GOLDEN DOME OF THE BIBLE

Without the Book of Revelation the Bible would be as incomplete as a building without a roof. Many subjects considered in preceding Scriptures would be left unanswered, out in the open and begging for proper coverage.

In fact, the Book of Revelation, with nearly 400 references and allusions (as pointed out by H.S. Miller in *General Biblical Introduction*), gives a finished covering for a great variety of subjects in twenty-five Old Testament books. What a remarkable testimony to the unity of the Bible! This short chapter will not permit one to take up these hundreds of references. Only some from Genesis will be considered here. This study will demonstrate this intriguing unity between Genesis and Revelation—a unity so thrilling that one must conclude that these two books, so widely separated in time, must have been inspired from the same Source!

Note first that Genesis 1:1–19 describes the creation of the earth and the heavens. But the last part of Revelation describes the destruction of that earth and heavens and unveils the creation of a wholly new earth and new heavens (21:1).

Genesis 3 marks the entrance of Satan into man's activities, but Revelation 20:10 gives Satan's final eternal fate in the lake of fire.

Genesis 1:26–31 describes the creation of man and woman in the beauty and purity of the divine image. But from Genesis 3 through Revelation 20 one repeatedly sees the awful downward degeneration of man; but the last two chapters of Revelation portray the glorious restoration of man to his former state. Hence, the whole story of man's history in the Bible can be covered with three words: *creation, degeneration,* and *restoration.* Truly this glorious restoration of man in Revelation gives the finishing touch, the golden dome for all the preceding books of the Bible. How incomplete, how lacking that finished touch the Bible would be without the Book of Revelation!

In Genesis 2:17 God warned man that if he ate the fruit of the tree of the knowledge of good and evil he would surely die. Because Adam and Eve wanted no restrictions on their freedom, they ate of the forbidden fruit. On that very day they began to die physically, mentally, and morally. Through all the ages since, Adam's descendants knew that every passing day brought them nearer to the dust from which they came.

Genesis introduced death to the human race. But Revelation 20:14 joyfully declares that death will also be destroyed in the lake of fire along with its Satanic originator.

Genesis also describes the beginnings of pain, sorrow, tears, lying, and murder (Genesis 3:16–19; 4:8). These, too, have hounded mankind through all the millennia of history. Then one comes to Revelation and the start of a glorious new era.

> And God shall wipe away all tears from their eyes; and there shall be no more death, neither sorrow, nor crying, neither shall there be any more pain; for the former things are passed away. And he that sat upon the throne said, Behold I make all things new. (21:4,5 KJV)

The roof that Revelation puts on the Bible is like a golden dome that reflects cheer and hope to suffering man.

In Genesis, after the fall of man, one reads that even the ground was cursed, crops were blighted and dwarfed while thorns and thistles flourished. Man had to eat his bread salted with his sweat and tears (3:17–19). And in the last part of the twentieth century conditions are worsening as man increasingly pollutes the air, the ground, and the rivers.

But cheer up! Revelation predicts "a time when there will be no more curse" (22:3 KJV). Instead of millions of people drinking chlorinated diluted sewage from lakes and rivers as today, the Book of Revelation describes "a pure river of water of life, clear as crystal" (22:1 KJV).

No more thorns, thistles, tears, sweat, locusts, and blasted crops! No more pollution of air, earth, and water! What a glorious prospect for the child of God!

Genesis introduces the wonderful tree of life yielding a different fruit each month. Adam and Eve were permitted to eat of this tree. These fruits kept them healthy and gave them immortality as long as they ate the fruit. But when they ate of the forbidden fruit "of the tree of the knowledge of good and evil," God put them out of the garden so that they could not continue to eat of the tree of life and live forever in sophisticated wickedness (Genesis 3:22).

Genesis only tells how man lost his right to eat of the tree of life. But Revelation gives the magnificent sequel to that tragedy. Describing the heavenly home of the Christian, Revelation reads:

> . . . And the main street was pure transparent gold, like glass (21:21 LP). And he pointed out to me a river of pure Water of Life, clear as crystal . . .
>
> Coursing down the center of the main street. On each side of the river grew Trees of Life, bearing twelve crops of fruit, with a fresh crop each month; the leaves were used . . . to heal the nations. (21:21b; 22:1,2 LNT)

What a place! A vast boulevard paved with crystal clear gold. And through the center of the boulevard runs the lovely river of life. This river is lined on both sides with disease-healing trees of life, "bearing twelve fruits, a different kind for each month" (PHILLIPS). Mortal minds cannot imagine such beauty. It must be seen.

One glance around heaven and the mind may well reminisce, "Why did I ever grieve when my little girl left earth for a place like this? And why did I come so unwillingly to such beauty?"

> Blessed are they that do his commandments, that they may have right to the tree of life, and may enter in through the gates into the city. (22:14 KJV)

In Genesis 37:9, Israel is symbolized as the sun, moon, and twelve stars. Israel is also thus symbolized in Revelation 12:1,5. This parallelism is most remarkable since the Revelation passage is devoid of the hallmarks of copyism.

In Genesis one notes a very special river that gives life-giving water to everything in God's garden in the land of Eden:

> From Eden a river flowed to water the park, which on leaving
> the park branched into four streams. (Genesis 2:10 MOFFATT)

After the fall one sees no mention of this great river. Scholars cannot locate it or be sure of the identity of some of its branches. Upheavals of the earth have changed the topography of the area.

But Revelation's description of the New Earth gives the counterpart of Eden's great river:

> And he pointed out to me a river of pure Water of Life, clear
> as crystal, flowing from the throne of God and the Lamb,
> coursing down the center of the main street. . . . (22:1,2 LNT)

Continue the study of the unity of Genesis and Revelation. In Genesis 1:3–5 light is created on the first day of creation. Yet the sun, moon, and stars were not made until the fourth day (1:16). How could there be light before the sun, moon, and stars? Some puzzled commentators assume that these heavenly bodies had to be created on the first day, even though the record clearly states that they were not made until the fourth day.

This paradox is understandable if one recalls the remarkable parallelism existing between Genesis and Revelation. Just as Genesis clearly states that there was *light* before the creation of the sun, moon, and stars, similarily Revelation predicts that there will be light after sun, moon, and stars have all passed away. What is more, Revelation gives the Source of that light:

> And the city has no need of sun or moon to light it, for the
> glory of God and of the Lamb illuminate it. (21:23 LNT)
> Its light will light the nations of the earth. . . . (v.24) and
> there is no night! (v.25)

The sun, moon, and stars of today have two other functions according to Genesis 1:14: ". . . for signs, and for seasons, and for days, and years." These latter statements have astronomical meaning. Day and night result from the rotation of the earth on its axis. A year is the time that it takes the earth to revolve around the sun. The seasons result from that revolution plus the fact that the earth's axis is inclined to the plane of its orbit.

Genesis 1:14 gives a third function of sun, moon, and stars (including planets): "for signs." Here is an important Scriptural subject, yet one that is practically unexplored. Those who would shy away from this field should remember that a star was the sign that showed the wise men the time of Jesus' birth and also led them to the place where He was. One must acknowledge that this incident was one fulfillment of Genesis 1:14.

Have there been any others? This writer submits certain facts that are well known but have never been correlated as far as he knows. The first point to consider: *On February 28, 1940, all of the five planets visible to the naked eye were visible as evening stars.* In the *Wheaton Record* Dr. Hawley O. Taylor wrote that Davis, then president of the Astronomical Society of Kansas City, had stated that the last time these five planets were visible at the same time was 2349 B.C. This date is approximately the time of the Flood. Various authorities give it as 2349, 2348, and 2347 B.C. No one knows the exact date. But one can say that the last time this most unusual heavenly phenomenon occurred was approximately the time of the Flood.

While doing research, I was intrigued with an article in the February 26, 1940, issue of *Life* describing this rare astronomical display. It stated that astronomers doubted if this was a sign of impending doom.

In my own mind I wondered. After reading the article and looking at the planetarium photograph showing all the planets in a line, I happened to glance at the large photograph on the facing page. It showed Jews walking in the gutters of a street in Warsaw, Poland, because Hitler ordered it. On their backs were prominent yellow·triangles, to get Jews marked for the slaughter that was just beginning.

The second point to contemplate: At the very time that this most unusual phenomenon took place, Hitler had marked every Jew for the greatest and the most ghastly massacre of all history—the extermination of 6 million of God's chosen people. Was this starry phenomenon a sign, a portent of impending disaster? Or was it a coincidence that the two times that this heavenly phenomenon was seen in all history just happened to occur before the two most awful calamities of all history?

Continuing the study of the parallelism between Genesis and Revelation one discovers that in Genesis 1:10 the seas were made. But for the rest of that story one has to read Revelation 21:1:

181

And I saw a new heaven and a new earth: for the first
heaven and the first earth were passed away; and there was
no more sea. (KJV)

In Genesis 15:18 the Euphrates River is Israel's boundary as prom-
ised by Jehovah. Much is made of this boundary elsewhere
(Deuteronomy 1:7; 11:24; Joshua 1:4; 2 Samuel 8:3; 1 Chronicles 18:3).
Even in Revelation 9:14 and 16:12 the spotlight is on the Euphrates
River as the border where a vast army of 200 million hesitates. They
are bound for Israel and the destruction of Jerusalem—so they think.
Actually they are headed for their own destruction at Armageddon.

Because the Euphrates River is so frequently given in Genesis and
elsewhere in the Old Testament as the eastern boundary of Israel, it
is possible that its two occurrences in Revelation indicate that this river
will be the eastern boundary of Israel in the last days. The Revelation
context lends support to such a view.

Some may wonder if Israel can extend her eastern border to the
Euphrates. Since Israel captured the Golan Heights in 1967, she would
have no trouble capturing Damascus lying about forty miles below in
a valley. Capture of this city would mean control of all the territory to
the Euphrates river.

In Genesis 3:24 one first sees the cherubim at the gate to the Garden
of Eden to keep man from continuing to eat of the tree of life. They
were acting as intermediaries between sinful man and a holy God. In
Revelation one also repeatedly sees the same cherubim repeatedly
acting as intermediaries between God and man (4:9–11; 5:8,14; 6:1–7;
15:7; 19:4–6).

In Genesis man had direct communion with God. But after the fall
man in the Old Testament could ordinarily only communicate with a
holy God through a priest in a tabernacle or a temple. But Revelation
predicts a time when direct, probably face to face, communion with
God will be restored:

And I heard a great voice out of heaven saying, Behold, the
tabernacle of God is with men, and he will dwell with them,
and they shall be his people, and God himself shall be with
them, and be their God.
And I saw no temple therein: for the Lord God Almighty and
the Lamb are the temple of it. (21:3,22 KJV)

Before the fall man was given rule over the earth (Genesis 1:28). But
after the fall "the prince of the power of the air" dominated. But

Revelation reveals a future day when man will reign with Christ over this earth (20:4; 22:5).

In Genesis 22:18 KJV the Lord promised Abraham, "And in thy seed [Christ] shall all the nations of the earth be blessed. . . ." Four times in Revelation the blessings that Christ gives to "every kindred, and tongue, and people, and nation are emphasized (5:9; 7:9; 10:11; 14:6).

In the first two chapters of Genesis the Father, Son, and Holy Spirit were blended and working together as a single unit. But with the fall of Adam, God gave up His own Son for man's redemption. A separation beyond human understanding took place. It reached its most awful depth and width when Jesus on the cross wailed, "My God, My God, why hast Thou forsaken Me?"

That separation that began in Genesis 3 does not entirely disappear until one comes to the last two chapters of Revelation. Not until then do the Father and Son lose their separate identities and blend into a homogeneous Person. There one discovers that, as in Genesis 1 and 2, again they are one—*one* temple, not two; *one* light, not two; and they occupy *one* throne, not two. (See *Guide*, Appendix 12 for details.)

Continuing the comparison of Genesis and Revelation, note that Genesis 10:2 gives the origin of Magog and that Ezekiel gives the location of Magog, Israel's future and final invader, as living in "the uttermost parts of the north." But it takes Revelation 20:7–10 to give the final fate of this utterly perverse and godless nation.

In Genesis 11 one reads how man in his pride built the Tower of Babel that became the center of idol worship. In Hebrew the name is *Babel* but in Greek it is *Babylon*. In Revelation 17 a great idol-worshipping church is also given the *symbolic* name of Babylon. It is given this symbolic name *Babylon* to identify it with its counterpart in Genesis. This apostate religion that began in Genesis is not finally destroyed until Revelation 17.

In Genesis not only did the people build an idolatrous tower but around it they also built a famous city (11:4,5). The people almost worshipped this city, wicked in many many ways. Genesis introduces one to Babylon but Revelation describes its destruction. Because of the wickedness of the whole country of Babylonia, God called Abraham out of it. He began to look for a much different kind of city—"a city which hath foundations, whose builder and maker is God" (Hebrews 11:10 KJV).

Genesis describes man's wicked city but Revelation describes God's city that Abraham sought. The city that Abraham yearned for in Genesis, the Apostle John saw and described in Revelation:

And I, John, saw the Holy City, the new Jerusalem, coming down from God out of heaven. It was a glorious sight, beautiful as a bride at her wedding. . . . (21:2 LNT)

It was filled with the glory of God, and flashed and glowed like a precious gem, crystal clear like jasper. . . . (v.11)

The angel held in his hand a golden measuring stick to measure the city and its gates and walls.

When he measured it, he found it was a square as wide as it was long; in fact, it was in the form of a cube, for its height was exactly the same as its other dimensions—1,500 miles each way. . . . (v.16) . . . the city itself was pure transparent gold, like glass! (v. 18)

The wall was made of jasper and was built on 12 layers of foundation stones inlaid with gems. . . . (adapted from vs.18–20)

The twelve gates were made of pearls—each gate from a single pearl! And the main street was pure transparent gold, like glass. (v.21)

This study of the wonderful Book of Revelation has now concluded with over a score of comparisons showing the inspired unity between Genesis and Revelation. As previously noted these references are only some of the nearly four hundred references that the Book of Revelation has with twenty-five Old Testament books. Is it not hard to imagine how any human author could possibly have written his own complicated descriptions of future events and at the same time have interwoven these hundreds of references into his own narration? All without any sign of the copyist! And all the references *adding* to and giving the finishing touches, often found nowhere else in the Bible!

There are more non-quotation references to the Old Testament found in Revelation than are found in all of the rest of the New Testament books combined! There must be a reason.

To any analytical reader it seems that the only logical way to explain the miraculous structure of this book is to believe the claim of its opening sentence, "This is a Revelation from Jesus Christ . . ." (PHILLIPS).

Then one can also understand why there is a special blessing to those who read and heed its message (Revelation 1:3). And one can also discern why there is a special curse placed on those who add to or subtract from the message of this book (22:18,19). There are rich rewards for those who *discern these times* with the illumination of His wonderful word.

A Study Guide to DISCERN THESE TIMES is forthcoming. This will contain questions, appendixes, and reference material with a comprehensive index. References to these appendixes are made throughout this volume, so that students will be better able to use the *Guide* in conjunction with *DISCERN THESE TIMES.*

BIBLIOGRAPHY

Alford, Henry. *The Greek New Testament.* Vol. 4. Boston: Lee and Shepard, 1880.

Anderson, Stanley E. *Our Dependable Bible.* Grand Rapids: Baker Book House, 1960.

Angeloglou, Christopher, and Haynes, Brian. *The Holy War June 6.* Banbury, England: Papers & Publications Ltd, 1967.

Aronow, Saul, *et al.*, eds. *The Fallen Sky.* New York: Hill and Wang, 1963.

Barclay, William. *The Revelation of John.* Philadelphia: Westminister Press, 1959.

Barker, Ernest. *From Alexander to Constantine.* London: Oxford University Press, 1956.

Baron, David. *The Visions and Prophecies of Zechariah.* London: Hebrew Christian Testimony to Israel, 1951.

Basseches, N. *Stalin.* New York: E. P. Dutton Co., 1952.

Bell, J. Bowyer. *The Long War.* Englewood Cliffs, N. J.: Prentice-Hall, Inc., 1969.

Blanshard, Paul. *American Freedom and Catholic Power.* Boston: Beacon Press, 1949.

——. *Freedom and Catholic Power in Spain and Portugal.* Boston: Beacon Press, 1962.

——. *Paul Blanshard on Vatican II.* Boston: Beacon Press, 1966.

Bondy, Ruth, *et al. Mission Survival.* New York: Sabra Books, Funk & Wagnalls, 1968.

Burnham, James. *The Struggle for the World.* New York: John Day Co., 1947.

Cadoux, Cecil John. *Catholicism and Christianity.* New York: Dial Press, 1929.

Calder, Nigel, ed. *Unless Peace Comes.* New York: Viking Press, 1968.

Chambers, Whittaker. *Witness.* New York: Random House, 1952.

Charles, R. H., ed. *The Apocrypha and Pseudepigrapha.* Vol. 2. New York: Oxford University Press, 1913.

Churchill, Winston. *A History of the English Speaking Peoples.* New York: Dodd, Mead & Co., 1956.

Clarke, Adam. *Clarke's Commentary.* 6 vols. Nashville: Abingdon-Cokesbury Press, n.d.

Desk Reference on Drug Abuse. Albany, N. Y.: New York State Department of Health, 1970, p. 10.

Einstein, Albert. *Ideas and Opinions.* New York: Crown Publishers, 1954.

Erdman, Charles R. *Revelation of John.* Philadelphia: Westminister Press, 1929.

Fraser, Alexander. *The Return of Christ in Glory.* Pittsburgh: The Evangelical Fellowship, 1947.

Friedlander, Saul. *Pope Pius XII and the Third Reich.* New York: Alfred A. Knopf, Inc., 1966.

Garrison, Winfred Ernest. *Catholicism and the American Mind.* Chicago: Willett, Clark and Colby, 1928.

Goodman and Gilman. *The Pharmacological Basis of Therapeutics.* New York: Macmillan Co., 1965.

Gretzinger, Harold W., *Atomic Bomb.* Long Beach, Calif.: Sacred Record of the Month Club, 1948.

Halley, Henry H. *Pocket Bible Handbook.* Chicago: Henry H. Halley, 1946.

Hendricksen, W. *More Than Conquerors.* Grand Rapids: Baker Book House, 1960.

Hilberg, Paul. *Destruction of the European Jews.* Chicago: Quadrangle Books, 1961.

Hochhuth, Rolf. *The Deputy.* New York: Grove Press, 1964.

Horne, Edward H. *The Meaning of the Apocalypse.* London: S.W. Partridge & Co., 1916.

Jamieson, R., ed. *Jamieson, Fausset & Brown's Commentary on the Whole Bible.* Grand Rapids: Zondervan Publishing House, n.d.

Josephus, Flavius. *Antiquities of the Jews.* Vol. 6. Cambridge, Mass.: Harvard University Press, 1958.

———. *The Works of Flavius Josephus.* Philadelphia: Porter and Coates, n.d.

Kac, Arthur W. *The Rebirth of the State of Israel—Is It of God or of Men?* Chicago: Moody Press, 1958.

Kavaler, Lucy. *Mushrooms, Molds, and Miracles.* New York: John Day Co., 1965.

Ladd, George E. *The Blessed Hope.* Grand Rapids: Wm. B. Eerdmans Publishing Co., 1956.

———. *The Gospel of the Kingdom.* Grand Rapids: Wm. B. Eerdmans Publishing Co., 1959.

La Pira, Giorgio, *et al. The Philosophy of Communism.* New York: Fordham University Press, 1952.

Larkin, Clarence. *The Book of Daniel.* Philadelphia: Erwin W. Moyer Co., 1929.

Lewy, Guenter. *The Catholic Church and Nazi Germany.* New York: McGraw-Hill Co., 1964.

Lilje, Hanns. *The Last Book of the Bible.* Philadelphia: Fortress Press, 1967.

Lindsey, Hal. *The Late Great Planet Earth.* Grand Rapids: Zondervan Publishing House, 1970.

McMillen, S.I. *None of These Diseases.* Old Tappan, N. J.: Fleming H. Revell Co., 1963.

Manhattan, Avro. *Vatican Imperialism in the Twentieth Century.* Grand Rapids: Zondervan Publishing House, 1965.

Marx, Karl. *The Civil War in France.* New York: International Publisher, 1937.

Maunder, E. W. *International Standard Bible Encyclopaedia.* Vol. 1. Grand Rapids: Wm. B. Eerdmans Publishing Co., 1946.

Miller, H. S. *General Biblical Introduction.* 9th ed. Houghton, N. Y.: The Word Bearer Press, 1956.

Miller, Irving. *Israel, the Eternal Ideal.* New York: H. Wolff, 1955.

Pache, Rene. *The Return of Jesus Christ.* Chicago: Moody Press, 1955.

Payne, J. Barton. *The Imminent Appearing of Christ.* Grand Rapids: Wm. B. Eerdmans Publishing Co., 1962.

Pfeiffer, Charles F., and Vos, Howard F. *The Wycliffe Historical Geography of Bible Lands.* Chicago: Moody Press, 1967.

Phillips, J. B. *The Book of Revelation.* New York: Macmillan Co., 1957.

Porter, H. *The International Standard Encyclopaedia.* Grand Rapids: Wm. B. Eerdmans Publishing Co., 1946.

Robertson, A. T. *Word Pictures in the New Testament.* New York: Harper Bros., 1933.

Roth, Cecil. *History of the Jews.* rev. ed. New York: Schocken Books, 1961.

Saint Augustine. *The City of God.* Translated by John Healey. London: J. M. Dent & Sons, 1931.

Scofield, C. I., ed. *Scofield Reference Bible.* New York: Oxford University Press, 1909.

Seiss, J. A. *The Apocalypse.* Grand Rapids: Zondervan Publishing House, n.d.

Skousen, W. Cleon. *The Naked Communist.* Salt Lake City: Ensign Publishing Co., 1961.

Smith, J. B. *A Revelation of Jesus Christ.* Scottdale, Pa.: Mennonite Publishing House, 1961.

Smith, Wilbur. *World Crises and the Prophetic Scriptures.* Chicago: Moody Bible Institute, 1950.

Starr, Chester G. *Civilization and the Caesars.* New York: W. W. Norton, 1965.

Story of the Bible World. Pleasantville, N. Y.: Reader's Digest Assn., n.d.

Stuart, John Leighton. *Fifty Years in China.* New York: Random House, 1955.

Swete, H. B. *The Apocalypse of John.* New York: Macmillan Co., 1909.

Talbot, Louis T. *The Revelation of Jesus Christ.* Grand Rapids: Wm. B. Eerdmans Publishing Co., 1908.

Tenny, Merrill C. *Interpreting Revelation.* Grand Rapids: Wm. B. Eerdmans Publishing Co., 1957.

Toynbee, Arnold J. *Civilization on Trial.* New York: Oxford University Press, 1948.

Uris, Leon. *Exodus.* New York: Doubleday & Co., 1959.

Vogt, Hannah. *The Burden of Guilt.* New York: Oxford University Press, 1964.

Walvoord, John F. *The Revelation of Jesus Christ.* Chicago: Moody Press, 1966.

Watts, Newman. *The Incomparable Book.* Surrey, England: Uplift Books, 1946.

Wesley, John. *Explanatory Notes Upon the New Testament.* London: Epworth Press, 1948.

West, Nathaniel. *The Thousand Years in Both Testaments.* New York: Fleming H. Revell, 1880.

World Almanac, The, and Book of Facts. New York: Newspaper Enterprise Assn., 1970, p. 554.

Young, Robert. *Analytical Concordance of the Bible.* New York: Funk & Wagnalls Co., n.d.

PERIODICALS

"Addiction-Connected Crime Deemed Major Law Problem." *The Attack,* Spring, 1969.

"At the U.N. behind the Pope's visit," *Christianity Today,* October 22, 1965 p. 37.

Buffalo (New York) Evening News, October 10, 1965; May 10, 1969; February 23, 1970; April 20, 1970.

Business Week, September 10, 1966, p. 90.

Carroll, Raymond. "The U. N. and Israel: 'The Deck Is Stacked.' " *Newsweek* (Educational Division), January, 1969.

"Drug Abuse: the Chemical Cop-out." *National Association of Blue Shield Plans,* April, 1969, p. 24.

Eisenhower, Dwight D. State of the Union Message, January, 1955.

Elliot, Elizabeth. Christian Herald, April, 1969, p. 20.

Graham, Billy. "The Life in the Blood." *Decision,* April, 1970.

Gretzinger, Harold W. "No Time to Waste." *Christian Life,* February, 1949.

Hekimian and Gershon. "Characteristics of Drug Abusers." *Journal of the American Medical Association,* July 15, 1968.

Kauffman, Donald. "Dateline Tomorrow." *Christian Herald,* August, 1969.

Kaufman, Philip K. "Eyeball to Eyeball Confrontation with Abuses Prevalent Among our Youth." *New York State Journal of Medicine,* September 15, 1969.

Levin, Max, M.D. *CMD,* April, 1970, pp. 374–377.

Louria, Donald B. "Drug Abuse: a Current Assessment." *AFP/GP,* June, 1970, p. 76.

Loyd, F. Glen, and Irwin, Theodore. "How Quackery Thrives on the Occult." *Today's Health,* Vol. 48 (November, 1970).

Lunarcharsky, Anatole. As quoted in U. S. *Congressional Record,* Vol. 77, pp. 1539–1540.

Medical World News, September 4, 1970, p. 15

"Megaton or Manger." *Christianity Today,* December 8, 1961.

Pillard, Richard C. "Marihuana." *New England Journal of Medicine,* August 6, 1970.

"Proliferating Problem." *MD,* September, 1970, p. 102.

Taylor, Dr. Hawley O. "Jupiter and Saturn" *Wheaton Record,* February 2, 1941.

Time, May 21, 1965, p. 35; January 5, 1968, p. 62.

Velie, Lester, "Countdown in the Holy Land." *Reader's Digest,* November, 1968.

Weil, Andrew T. "Adverse Reactions to Marihuana." *New England Journal of Medicine,* April 30, 1970.

A Study Guide to DISCERN THESE TIMES is forthcoming. This will contain questions, appendixes, and reference material with a comprehensive index. References to these appendixes are made throughout this volume, so that students will be better able to use the *Guide* in conjunction with *DISCERN THESE TIMES.*